Also by Omar El Akkad

American War
What Strange Paradise

ONE
DAY,
EVERYONE
WILL
HAVE
ALWAYS
BEEN
AGAINST
THIS

ONE
DAY,
EVERYONE
WILL
HAVE
ALWAYS
BEEN
AGAINST
THIS

Omar El Akkad

Alfred A. Knopf   New York   2025

www.aaknopf.com

Knopf, Borzoi Books, and the colophon are registered
trademarks of Penguin Random House LLC.

"poem for brad who wants me to write about the pyramids," by Marwa Helal
from *Invasive species* (Nightboat Books, 2019). Reprinted with permission.

Library of Congress Cataloging-in-Publication Data
Names: El Akkad, Omar, 1982– author.
Title: One day, everyone will have always been against this / Omar El Akkad.
Identifiers: LCCN 2024035282 (print) | LCCN 2024035283 (ebook) |
ISBN 9780593804148 (hardcover) | ISBN 9780593804155 (ebook) |
ISBN 9781524712815 (open market)
Subjects: LCSH: El Akkad, Omar, 1982– | Arab American authors—Biography. |
Journalists—United States—Biography. | Israel-Hamas War, 2023– | Muslims—
United States—Social conditions. | Arabs—United States—Social conditions.
Classification: LCC PS3605.L12 Z46 2025 (print) | LCC PS3605.L12 (ebook) |
DDC 813/.6—dc23/eng/20241031
LC record available at https://lccn.loc.gov/2024035282
LC ebook record available at https://lccn.loc.gov/2024035283

Jacket illustration by Ahmad Sabbagh
Jacket design by Janet Hansen

Manufactured in the United States of America

First Edition

"Sooner or later they will leave our country, just as many people throughout history left many countries. The railways, ships, hospitals, factories and schools will be ours and we'll speak their language without either a sense of guilt or a sense of gratitude. Once again we shall be as we were—ordinary people—and if we are lies we shall be lies of our own making."

—Tayeb Salih, *Season of Migration to the North*

"Are those your children?" "Yes."

—Wisława Szymborska, "Vietnam" (trans. Stanisław Barańczak and Clare Cavanagh)

CONTENTS

ONE
DAY,
EVERYONE
WILL
HAVE
ALWAYS
BEEN
AGAINST
THIS

She is fog-colored when they find her, she believes she has ended. Like porters in service of some grotesque nobility, half a dozen men carry the stretcher out of something cavernous, something that used to be a home, and she, a girl of nine or ten, is whisked away. Sitting on the stretcher, dazed and bloodied, she looks off to the side. She appears to be searching. The men who carry the stretcher move with urgency, as if the doing of care, of gentleness, can undo what has happened to this girl, to this place, to the bodies yet to be dug from beneath the rubble. Someone nearby asks God for revenge. Perhaps God is here somewhere, also searching.

    A soldier I met years ago, who made the study of industrial violence his hobby, once told me the first thing that kills when a bomb goes off isn't shrapnel or fire. It's the overpressure wave: air forced violently outward from the site of the blast. What you're supposed to do, he said, is drop to the ground and cover your ears, breathe out, empty your lungs before the air collides with and flattens them. Of course, if you're close enough, nothing you

*do or don't do will make any difference at all. He said the force of
the overpressure wave weakens in proportion to the cube of the
distance from the site of impact, which is to say, the most effective
thing you can do to avoid getting killed by a missile or a mine or
a grenade is to be far away when it goes off.*

How do you do that? I asked.

Do what?

*Know when a thing like that is about to happen. Know to be
far away.*

*Well, he said, and trailed off. A few minutes later he was
telling the story of a freak accident his daughter had suffered as a
toddler, how carrying her to the emergency room was the scariest
thing he'd ever experienced. Even in his line of work, even with all
he'd seen, the scariest thing.*

*As the men carry the girl out of what used to be her home, she
asks if they're going to take her to the cemetery. One of the men
says,* Mashallah, mashallah.

*In literal translation, the word means: What God wills. A
closer approximation of meaning—of one meaning—is something
like: What has happened is what God willed. But English, tasked
with a word like this, turns stiff and monophonic, and* Mashallah
*is orchestral. To any ear that grew up on this language, it is clear
that what the man means when he says this word is something
else entirely. Something instantly familiar to generations who've
heard it spilling out of the mouths of beaming grandmothers
at the end of piano recitals and graduation ceremonies and at
the first sight of a newborn. Used this way, it finds its principal*

purpose, as an expression of joy. Look at this wonderful thing
God has done.

ما شاء الله

Language, too, forces the air from the lungs.

Beyond the high walls and barbed wire and checkpoints
that pen this place, there is the empire. And the empire as well
is cocooned inside its own fortress of language—a language
through the prism of which buildings are never destroyed but
rather spontaneously combust, in which blasts come and go like
Chinooks over the mountain, and people are killed as though
to be killed is the only natural and rightful ordering of their
existence. As though living was the aberration. And this language
might protect the empire's most bloodthirsty fringe, but the fringe
has no use for linguistic malpractice. It is instead the middle, the
liberal, well-meaning, easily upset middle, that desperately needs
the protection this kind of language provides. Because it is the
middle of the empire that must look upon this and say: Yes, this
is tragic, but necessary, because the alternative is barbarism. The
alternative to the countless killed and maimed and orphaned
and left without home without school without hospital and the
screaming from under the rubble and the corpses disposed of
by vultures and dogs and the days-old babies left to scream and
starve, is barbarism.

The girl on the stretcher believes she has ended. A man says to
her: Inti zay el amar.

You are like the moon. Again, translation fails. There is no English equivalent to the lineage of this phrase, a lineage that runs through generations of old movies and love songs and family gatherings. Listen to the sly setting joy and pleading, raw pleading that carries the words as this man tells the girl who lived when so many others died that she is beautiful beyond the bounds of this world.

زي القمر

Something has ended here. But something else begins. The dead dig wells in the living.

CHAPTER ONE

DEPARTURE

An eighteen-month-old with a bullet wound to the forehead.
Maybe the sniper was aiming elsewhere. Maybe there's some
explanation. Maybe it was necessary.

Portland, 2024:

Spring, nearing. My daughter has been building a city. Its Main
Street runs the length of our hallway, from the front door to
the dining room. She unspools a long sheet of paper and draws
lane dividers and sidewalks, trees and shrubbery. Along the
wall, near the little marks we've used to document her height
since she could first stand, she has cut out and placed little
storefronts made of pink and orange construction paper:
supermarkets and coffee shops, a pet store. At the end of the
road, at least a dozen stuffed animals sit solemnly within the
confines of what I can only imagine is some kind of planned
community. My daughter arranges them just so, gives each
its space, starts building them a park. She turns seven soon, a
hundred in dragon years. She is made of dreaming.

We live in the woods in Oregon. Wine and hazelnut country, somewhere in that strange middle space past where progressive Portland ends but before Trump Country begins. A year before my daughter was born, we tried to find a house in the city, couldn't afford anything, and ended up looking further and further out. We spent weeks traversing all these little outposts on the east and north sides of the Willamette Valley, and across the Columbia River in southernmost Washington. After vetoing two other neighborhoods on account of Confederate flags flying in nearby yards, we landed here, next door to a World War II veteran on one side and, for a brief stretch of about three months, some guy who thought a home on a rural road with no sidewalks in the middle of nowhere, serenaded near-nightly by a chorus of coyotes, would make for a good Airbnb property. He sold after a couple of months.

This is the sixteenth or seventeenth home I've lived in, I'm not entirely sure. But it's my children's first. In stable orbit their lives spin around this house, this town, this country—some 7,000 miles from the places where their father's childhood first came undone.

Occasionally I show them pictures, crack open my now-arthritic high school yearbook and say, yes, that's me with the ridiculous curls, with a full head of hair. I show them pictures of their grandfather, who died before either of them were born. In one photo he's parked on the side of a desert road next to his friend's car. Both of them are driving those lean, early-'90s Mercedes sedans. I try to explain to a couple of children who

8

have no idea what the hell I'm talking about that these cars were *the* status symbol of the time, proof my family had joined the ranks of the upper middle class. I see their eyes start to glaze over and all at once I'm struck by the absurdity—how did any of this ever seem important? I was roughly the same age my daughter is now when my dad got that Mercedes. I remember yelping. I did a little dance.

There's an unbridgeable distance. I know it, and I think my children can already sense it. I tell my daughter one day I'll take her to the place I was born, and she can see the pyramids for herself, figure out what's really going on with the Sphinx's nose. I tell her about the beaches along the north coast where the coral's neon bright and you can swim right up and pet the fishies. I warn her it won't be like anything she's experienced before. You know how people stop at red lights here? I ask. Well, when we get there, don't be surprised if . . . I pause, try to figure out how to prepare a child for what, relative to all she's known so far in life, would come across as complete chaos. People there have made a language out of honking horns, I say, and she laughs, and I know deep down I might never take her back.

I've learned to justify it to myself, this severance. It'll overwhelm her, confuse her, and anyway, I've been gone so long from the country of my blood that there's really no point, no connection left. But there's a fraudulence to those excuses, no different than when my wife and I found out we were having a girl, and I spent weeks and weeks considering baby names that would work in the West and the Middle East, that would allow her to pass through many worlds untroubled.

In truth, I lean away from the faraway side of my daughter's lineage on her behalf because for more than forty years I've seen what carrying that weight means. I've seen cousins pulled into secondary at JFK on account of their Arabic accents; I've heard my own name mangled every which way, the letter ع turning to syrup in the throat if you haven't been brought up hearing and saying it. I've explained, politely, to deeply well-meaning people that I don't have a problem shaking hands with women—maybe other Muslims do, I couldn't tell you; we don't all know each other. I've sat through a wildly uncomfortable book tour interview once after I joked that I write all my novels in Arabic and then run them through Google Translate, and the interviewer believed me. I have on countless occasions been made to stand in for and speak on behalf of every Muslim, every Arab, every Brown person on earth, by people who are not monsters, not even actively malicious, but simply have no other point of reference to consult. I've smiled and nodded. I was nice about it.

None of this matters much, in the grand scheme of things. I've learned to deal with it—but why should she? In truth, I keep a distance between who my daughter is and what she comes from because it'll be easier for her that way.

Which is to say, because I'm a coward.

My daughter pauses, midway through drawing the Vs of a swing set in the park of her stuffies' imaginary suburb. She gets up, walks over to where I'm sitting in the living room scrolling through photographs and videos taken in the aftermath of yet another atrocity in Gaza. She wants to double-check the spelling of "Welcome."

I shut my computer, quickly. In various browser tabs, there is footage of a girl not much older than my daughter, pulled out of the rubble after an Israeli airstrike. In another is a recording of a girl begging for help, shortly before her execution at the hands of Israeli snipers. I have more than twenty tabs open, a bloody carnival of the worst crimes ever livestreamed. I tell my daughter she's spelled the word correctly. She returns to her park, light as air.

●

I am in possession of this, my first memory of war:

Autumn, 1990; third grade. The American International School in Doha, Qatar, was founded by the U.S. ambassador. His posting, I assume, came as such things do, a reward for some sufficiently large campaign donation. The AIS was built in part for his daughter, G., on whom I had my very first crush.

That fall, feeding on stray crumbs of adult conversation—things said indiscreetly just within earshot, the nightly news in the other room—I learned there was a war about to begin. Not here, but nearby. I remember watching my father place big Xs of duct tape across all our balcony windows, supposedly to keep them from shattering in the event of a blast. He made jokes about it, and I realize now it was to keep his son calm, to paint as trivial a thing that, had it come, would not be.

Still, we knew we were not in the middle of this war, the air would not be pushed out of our lungs. Quickly, the conflict eventually known as the Gulf War, and later the First Gulf War, transformed from a thing no one talked about to a normal mechanic of everyday life, no different than humidity or dusk. The endless footage on CNN that at first provoked such shock—these shadowed Baghdad cityscapes detonating sporadically in balls of pale white light—soon caused no reaction at all. It was just what happened to certain places, to certain people: they became balls of pale white light. What mattered was, it wasn't us.

During the First Gulf War, the Americans arrived. There had been plenty of Americans before then, of course, plenty of expats from all over. (In the hierarchy of migration, "expat" is largely reserved for white Westerners who leave their homes for another country, usually because the money's better there. When other people do this, they might be deemed "aliens" or "illegals" or at best "economic migrants." As with most criteria of segregation, everyone knows, instinctively, how they will be labeled. It's a matter of self-preservation, to know.) Qatar being home to some of the largest natural gas reserves on earth, it had for decades attracted foreigners looking for a life that, if you've never lived it, feels almost unreal. A life in which multiple housemaids and drivers and villas are not exclusive to the wealthiest few, but the normal trappings of upper-middle-class life. At the time I lived there, about 90 percent of Qatar's residents were non-Qatari. Of these, most were "third country" laborers—people who had come from Pakistan and India and the Philippines and Bangladesh and Nepal (and, later, most every part of sub-Saharan Africa) to drive the cars and build the towers and clean the villas. It was on the backs of these people that much of the oil-rich Arabian Gulf was constructed and, to this day, they are afforded almost no rights at all, no ownership of the glittering fantasy that fossil fuel profits paid for and the bodies of these men and women made real.

But the Americans who showed up during the war had not come to live in the villas and work in the office towers. They occupied a small mess of tents on the outskirts of the city. They wore military fatigues, they looked like the Americans we'd seen in movies and on television. In class, our teacher had us write them thank-you letters that were later delivered to the base. I don't remember what I was supposed to be grateful for, only that gratitude was important. That without these people, and what they were willing to do, the world would be a very different place.

■

Four years earlier, my father, then only thirty-one and working in the accounting department at the Cairo Sheraton in Egypt, was leaving the hotel one night when a couple of soldiers decided to give him a hard time.

The country was still sleepwalking through the ugly years following the assassination of President Anwar El-Sadat. After signing the Camp David Accords, formalizing peace between Egypt and Israel, Sadat was shot to death during a military parade in 1981 by an Islamic fundamentalist military officer. Of the few impressions of Egypt I suspect I share with my father, who has been dead now more than a decade, there is this sense that, more often than not, for people who are from the places we're from, power changes hands this way: a killing, a coup, a successful revolution, a failed revolution. My father loved Egypt. He knew it for exactly what it was and loved it still.

Shortly after I was born, in 1982, the man who killed Sadat went before the firing squad, and for years the whole country lived under the suffocating gravity of martial law. To be outside at night required a formal reason, or else one risked harassment by the soldiers who seemed to make a military checkpoint out of every intersection. It is a hallmark of failing societies, I've learned, this requirement that one always be in possession of a valid reason to exist.

It was late, my father was done work for the night. Because he was technically part of the tourism industry, and the Egyptian economy has for a very long time depended on tourism to ward off complete collapse, he was afforded special dispensation to be out during curfew hours. The soldiers on the corner did not know this. Young, bored, tasked with what authoritarian regimes have ordered young, bored soldiers to do since time immemorial—stand there projecting the violent underpinning of political power—they also didn't care. One of them stopped my father.

Your papers, he said.

My father pulled out his paperwork. Without reading it, the soldier tore it in half and threw it on the floor.

Your papers, he repeated.

In the forty or so years since that day, I have thought about this moment more than anything else in the stories my father told me. I've thought about it while shuffling my passport across the counter at border crossings; while running from RPG attacks in the dead of night; while sitting in a guesthouse in Kandahar listening to two Taliban officials explain, with utmost confidence, how the world should be run; while sitting in a courtroom in Guantánamo Bay watching highly educated men and women assign legitimacy they know is unearned to an ad hoc, hopelessly compromised legal system. It has been, for as long as I can remember, the memory that anchors my overarching view of political malice: an ephemeral relationship with both law and principle. Rules, conventions, morals, reality itself: all exist so long as their existence is convenient to the preservation of power. Otherwise, they, like all else, are expendable.

By chance, my father's boss, who happened to be friends with one of the soldiers, was leaving the hotel a short while later and stumbled onto the scene. This is likely the only reason my father got out unscathed that night, avoided being dragged to some outpost of Egypt's labyrinthine secret prison system, being made into an absence. It was that night, I think, that my father decided he had no choice but to leave the only home he'd ever known.

He'd been flirting with departure a long time. Egypt, like so many places trying to forge a path on the other side of colonialism, was a country in which the future had been exiled, governed by people who provided for the vast majority of their citizens no plausible avenue of progress from one's current state to something better. Under foreign and then local rule, the central directive never changed: Know your place. It's a frequent, nauseating political inheritance: come to experience the world under the reign of someone who thinks of you as subhuman, as undeserving of a future, and an ugly impression is settled that true power is the ability to do the same to someone else. The foreigners had departed; there was no one left to do it to but our own.

And so one day my father, who loved Egypt, who had marinated in its music and poetry and knew every street, every alley, who as a child had sat under the tables at Hagg El Feshawy's coffee shop in El Hussein and listened to Naguib Mahfouz hold court decades before the Nobel, decided he needed to get out. Elsewhere has since been our lot to carry.

It was no unusual thing, for the likes of us to scatter. After a few months of looking, my father found a job abroad, the way so many Arab men did in those years and the years that followed. It was another accounting gig at a hotel in Libya. On the day his new life was supposed to begin, my father went to Cairo airport, handed his passport at security, and was promptly detained.

Naming conventions in much of the Arab world assign the father's first name as the son's middle name. My name is Omar Mohammed El Akkad. My father is Mohammed Ahmad El

Akkad. My grandfather, a clothing merchant who died a few months before my father was born and whose funeral, I'm told, brought all of El Hussein to a standstill, is Ahmad Suleyman El Akkad. Unfortunately for my father, the name "Mohammed Ahmad" is about as ubiquitous as exists anywhere. It happens that the same name pops up on a Libyan terrorism watchlist. He is taken into secondary screening. My father's age precludes him from being the same wanted man, but he's denied entry into Libya anyway. We never end up going.

Not long after, another job offer arrives. This time it's in a tiny peninsula called Qatar, a thoroughly ignored outpost of the British Empire that, not long before, had gained its independence and discovered massive fossil fuel deposits. It was one of the fastest-growing nations on the planet, flush with cash and in desperate need of workers. My father accepted a position at a hotel in the Qatari capital, Doha. He knew nothing about the place, had no desire to go beyond the money on offer. It paid better than anything he'd ever find in Egypt. (One of the more ironic facets of living in a place like Qatar— one of the safest nations on earth, at least from the middle class on up—is that so many people move to this place and are then granted a bonus, "hardship pay," for living outside their home countries.) He had a family to support. And so we left; have been leaving ever since.

One of the hallmarks of Western liberalism is an assumption, in hindsight, of virtuous resistance as the only polite expectation of people on the receiving end of colonialism. While the terrible thing is happening—while the

17

land is still being stolen and the natives still being killed—any form of opposition is terroristic and must be crushed for the sake of civilization. But decades, centuries later, when enough of the land has been stolen and enough of the natives killed, it is safe enough to venerate resistance in hindsight. I tell stories for a living, and there's a thick thread of narrative by well-meaning white Westerners that exalts the native populations in so many parts of the world for standing up to the occupiers, makes of their narrative a neat reflexive arc in which it was always understood, by the colonized and (this part implied) the descendants of the colonizer, that what happened was wrong.

It's a comforting thing, this narrative, and at my most susceptible to whatever the West is, I want so dearly to partake in it. But it's a fiction, the most malicious kind: a fiction of moral convenience. Some, maybe most, might resist the wanting whims of empire, but all must figure out a way to survive them. And survival is not clean, does not subscribe to any one narrative. For every victim of colonialism who resisted, there might be another who, like countless members of my parents' and grandparents' generations, looked to the French and the British and thought: This is what winners look like. These are the languages they speak and these are the customs they practice and if our own children are to have any chance at all they must become fluent in these things because anything less than fluency is a sentence to a life of something lesser. It is this impulse, to give your child a fighting chance at privilege by immersing them in the myriad languages of the privileged world, that makes me who I am, that lands me in the American

International School at age eight, writing thank-you letters to American soldiers.

We are all governed by chance. We are all subjects of distance.

■

The winter I turned sixteen, my best friend Donny got his driver's license. There being not much to do in Doha during the late 1990s, we spent a lot of weekend nights driving around aimlessly—over to the drive-thru of the twenty-four-hour Dairy Queen, or the skeleton of that building by the Jedda overpass that was halted mid-construction when it became clear the residents in the upper floors would have an unobstructed view behind the walls of a sheikh's neighboring estate.

One night, near where the Ramada roundabout used to be (we lived in one of those places where absolutely nobody used street names or numbers, only landmarks), we came across a fender bender. Two cars were parked on the side of the road. The one that had been rear-ended, a Mercedes, belonged to a man who, by his clothing, was almost certainly a local. The driver of the Daewoo that had done the rear-ending was Southeast Asian, likely Indian or Pakistani. We drove slowly past them, gawking as the man in the Mercedes stormed out of the car and, in what seemed like one swift movement, removed one of his sandals, rushed over to the driver of the Daewoo, and started pummeling him with it. Traffic slowed, something of a communal spectacle quickly developed. Passing drivers honked their horns, some kids not much older than us rolled down their windows and yelled something, laughing hysterically. We watched, we laughed. The whole thing must have lasted at most fifteen seconds. And yet I've never stopped thinking about it, about the rage in one man's eyes and the fear in the other's.

It came to me, a long time later, that the Southeast Asian man had done something worse than dent a fancy car's bumper. He had violated the bounds of his assumed nonexistence. In this place, at this time, people who looked like him were to be invisible. They could perform labor and be paid wages, but as vessels of agency beyond the most necessary transactions, they quite simply did not exist. They were not subhuman, they were nonhuman, non-anything. To allow oneself to think otherwise risked having to contend with the reality that this whole place lived on top of people who looked just like this man. It risked an indictment of an entire narrative, a self-told story of being. It risked everything.

I return to the memory of that moment often, the way we watched and laughed, didn't think for a second to stop, to interfere, as the man in the Mercedes assaulted someone whose existence he had been so rudely forced to acknowledge. It's come to shape the way I think about every country, every community: Whose nonexistence is necessary to the self-conception of this place, and how uncontrollable is the rage whenever that nonexistence is violated?

■

Somewhere in the basement of my mother's house in Ottawa there's a CD rack I haven't touched in about a quarter century. It is, as you'd expect, a truly embarrassing archival tower of 1990s cultural ephemera: Meatloaf's second *Bat Out of Hell* album; the Letters to Cleo single with the near-indecipherable chorus; about half a dozen *Now That's What I Call Music!* compilations full of the worst, most earwormy Brit-pop ever conceived. Among this mess are two Nirvana records I played to death when I first got my hands on them: *Nevermind* and *In Utero.* (There were no real record stores in Qatar back in the 1980s and early '90s, only a small variety store of sorts on the ground floor of the Doha Sheraton that, occasionally and inexplicably, sold a random assortment of CDs.) On the cover of *Nevermind,* the naked baby in the pool has been blacked out by a government censor's marker; on the cover of *In Utero,* only the angel's head and wings are visible. Such was the experience of consuming culture throughout my adolescence, a tiring cat-and-mouse of books and films smuggled into the country from abroad at great personal risk, of magazines held up to the light bulb in the hopes of seeing through the black ink, of this impotent rage at some anonymous government hack who was deciding what was too dangerous for me to hear, to watch, to read. (I learned later that the chief government censor during those years was the mother of one of my closest friends—just the sweetest woman.) Brought up this way, I held on to the thought that elsewhere, in the part of the world where these books and films and songs that so shaped my life were made, things were different.

The mind outlines better than it shades. England, Canada, the United States, the West, these places—or rather ideas of places—became in my imagination the negative space of all I despised about the Middle East: the repression, the sheer docility expected of everyone on all matters political or social, the gaggle of idiot Dear Leaders whose embellished jawlines were plastered on most every vertical public surface. (I remember one visit back to Egypt where, upon leaving the airport and driving through the streets of Cairo, I looked out the window and saw a giant billboard with President Hosni Mubarak's beaming face drawn on it, and a note from a sycophantic businessman congratulating him on winning the election. The election was still four months away.) All I knew about the other side of the planet, all I needed to know, was that it wasn't like this. In the unfree world, the free world isn't a place or a policy or a way of living; it's a negation. National anthems and military flyovers and little flag lapel pins are all well and good, but for a life stunted by a particular kind of repression, the driving force will never be toward something better, but away from something worse. The harbor never as safe as the water is cold.

I wanted for that other place. I wanted for the part of the world where I believed there existed a fundamental kind of freedom. The freedom to become something better than what you were born into, the freedom that comes with an inherent fairness of treatment under law and order and social norm, the freedom to read and write and speak without fear. And more than any of these things, the freedom to be left alone.

It was an impulse that remained with me through the very dark years of my early adulthood. It remained even during the War on Terror years where, first as a college student and then for ten years as a journalist, I saw the terrible wrath of the place, saw it obliterate hundreds of thousands of people with names and ethnicity and religion like mine, knew for certain that there were deep ugly cracks in the bedrock of this thing called "the free world." And yet I believed the cracks could be fixed, that the thing at the core, whatever it was, was salvageable.

Until the fall of 2023. Until the slaughter.

Beginning in October of that year, the Israeli military, at the direction of the country's government and with the support of the vast majority of the Western world's political power centers, enacted a campaign of active genocide against the Palestinian people, one of the most openly, wantonly vicious campaigns in the near-century-long occupation, and easily the most well documented.

On October 7, 2023, armed groups led by Hamas's military wing launched a coordinated attack on multiple cities near the Israeli-occupied Gaza Strip. Fighters killed 1,195 people, of which 815 were civilians, according to an analysis by Agence France-Presse, including at least 282 women and 36 children. They abducted more than 250 people. It was a bloodbath, orchestrated by exactly the kind of entity that thrives in the absence of anything resembling a future.

Immediately afterward, Israel began a campaign of obliteration throughout Gaza. Almost all the region's

2.3 million residents have been displaced. Virtually every school, hospital, and university was either damaged or destroyed. The deliberate withholding of aid and destruction of infrastructure have resulted in widespread famine and death by disease. Over and over, residents were ordered from their neighborhoods into "safe zones" and then wiped out there. Some people are afforded precision in death, but not these: there is no accurate count of the murdered. There may never be.

When next this happens (and it will happen, again and again, because a people remain under occupation and because the relative compelling powers of both revenge and consequence warp beyond recognition once one has been made to bury their child), this same framing can always be used. The barbarians instigate and the civilized are forced to respond. The starting point of history can always be shifted, such that one side is always instigating, the other always justified in response.

Words exist only in hindsight; time passes over and around them like water along a canyon floor. In the year or so between when I write these words and when they are published, perhaps so many innocent people will have been killed, so many mass graves discovered, that it will not be so controversial to state plainly what is plainly known. But for now we argue, in this part of the world, the part not reduced to rubble, about how words make us feel. It's a kind of pastime. Almost every day an influential opinion columnist or think tank expert or spokesperson for the president of the United States will feign outrage at how hurtful words such as "genocide" and "occupation" are, how disparaging, how uncouth.

I have seen, almost daily, for months, images of children mutilated, starved to death, executed. Bodies in pieces. Parents burying limbs.

In time, there will be nothing particularly controversial about using these words to describe the things they were created to describe. (The very history of the word "genocide," meant as a mechanic of forewarning rather than some after-the-fact resolution, is littered with instances of the world's most powerful governments going to whatever lengths they can to avoid its usage, because usage is attached to obligation. It was never intended to be enough to simply call something genocide: one is required to act.) Once far enough removed, everyone will be properly aghast that any of this was allowed to happen. But for now, it's just so much safer to look away, to keep one's head down, periodically checking on the balance of polite society to see if it is not too troublesome yet to state what to the conscience was never unclear.

In the coming years there will be much written about what took place in Gaza, the horrors that have been meticulously documented by Palestinians as they happened and meticulously brushed aside by the major media apparatus of the Western world. As it stands, the death toll is quite literally uncountable—tens or hundreds of thousands of people, likely tens or hundreds of thousands more to be found under the rubble, or wasted away from disease and starvation imposed by an occupation force that seeks, actively and for all to see, their expulsion or else extermination. Here, when we name the dead, when we name *these* dead in particular, it is customary to note the number of children obliterated, because the men are assumed to be terrorists and the women might be terrorists or at the very least go on to create them. Whatever mainstream Western liberalism is—and I have no useful definition of it beyond something at its core transactional, centered on the magnanimous, enlightened image of the self and the dissonant belief that empathizing with the plight of the faraway oppressed is compatible with benefiting from the systems that oppress them—it subscribes to this calculus. People go to see the president in the White House for what they know is only a meaningless photo op and yet, in the hopes of getting him to see, to do something, anything, they show him pictures of the mangled bodies of children. It doesn't work. There is no transaction to be had; these dead kids offer nothing in return.

But this is not an account of that carnage, though it must in its own way address it, if only to uphold the most pathetic, necessary function of this work: witness. This is an account of something else, something that, for an entire generation of not just Arabs or Muslims or Brown people but rather all manner of human beings from all parts of the world, fundamentally changed during this season of completely preventable horror. This is an account of a fracture, a breaking away from the notion that the polite, Western liberal ever stood for anything at all.

—

To maintain belief in what is commonly called the rules-based order requires a tolerance for disappointment. It's not enough to subscribe to the idea that there exist certain inflexible principles derived from what in the parlance of America's founding documents might be called self-evident truths, and that the basic price of admission to civilized society is to do whatever is necessary to uphold these principles. One must also believe that, no matter the day-to-day disappointments of political opportunism or corruption or the cavalcade of anesthetizing lies that make up the bulk of most every election campaign, there is something solid holding the whole endeavor together, something greater. For members of every generation, there comes a moment of complete and completely emptying disgust when it is revealed there is only a hollow. A completely malleable thing whose primary use is not the opposition of evil or administration of justice but the preservation of existing power. History is a debris field of such moments. They arrive in the form of British and French soldiers to the part of the world I'm from. They come to the Salvadorans and Chileans and Iranians and Vietnamese and Cambodians in the form of toppled governments and coups over oil revenue and villages that had to be burned to the ground to save them from some otherwise terrible fate. They arrived at the turn of the twentieth century to Hawaii (the U.S. apologized for the overthrow of the Hawaiian government—almost a hundred years later). They come to the Indigenous population eradicated to make way for what would become the most powerful nation on earth, and to the Black population forced in chains to build it, severed from home such that, as James Baldwin said, every subsequent generation's search for lineage arrives, inevitably, not at a nation or a community, but a bill of sale. And at every moment of arrival the details and the body count may differ, but in the marrow there is always a commonality: an ambitious, upright, pragmatic voice saying, *Just for a moment, for the greater good, cease to believe that this particular group of people, from whose experience we are already so safely distanced, are human.*

Now, for a new generation, the same moment arrives. To watch the leader of the most powerful nation on earth endorse and finance a genocide prompts not a passing kind of disgust or anger, but a severance. The empire may claim fear of violence because the fear of violence justifies any measure of violence in return, but this severance is of another kind: a walking away, a noninvolvement with the machinery that would produce, or allow to produce, such horror. What has happened, for all the future bloodshed it will prompt, will be remembered as the moment millions of people looked at the West, the rules-based order, the shell of modern liberalism and the capitalistic thing it serves, and said: I want nothing to do with this.

Here, then, is an account of an ending.

CHAPTER TWO

WITNESS

In the pauses between onslaught, they arrive at what's left of the
hospitals, missing limbs, skin burned away, maggots crawling out
of the wounds. The medics are forced to create a new acronym for
them. WCNSF—Wounded Child, No Surviving Family.

Montreal, 1998:

For the first sixteen years of my life, I have no sense of what
winter can be.

Montreal is not a forgiving initiation. I remember standing
near the Roddick Gates on Sherbrooke Street, at the foot of
the McGill University campus, waiting on a friend. Early
December: the first really cold days. My parents and I had
only just arrived in Canada three months earlier. On my last
morning in Qatar, the temperature was set to reach a high
somewhere in the 40s Celsius, the 110s Fahrenheit. Now,
magnified by this thing called wind chill that I'd never heard
of before, Montreal dips to 30 or 40 below zero, where the
distinction between Celsius and Fahrenheit doesn't much

matter anymore. I stand on the sidewalk, trying to understand how anyone can live like this. I'd forgotten my hat at home; I cover my ears and shake my head, like someone refusing to hear bad news.

Immigration is barely a phenomenon of physical or cultural geography; the landscape marks the smallest change. In the Middle East I'd seen North Americans and Europeans arrive and immediately cocoon themselves into gated compounds and gated friendships. So normalized was this walling off that a Westerner could spend decades in a place like Qatar and only briefly contend with the inconvenience of their host nation's ways of living.

(It would come as a genuine surprise to me, years later, when I came to the West and found that this precise thing was a routine accusation lobbed at people from my part of the world. We simply did not do enough to learn the language, the culture. We stubbornly *refused to assimilate.*)

Instead, something else changes most radically in the psychology of someone who leaves home: a relative distance between the person one is and the person they must become. Westerners in Qatar left the smallness of past selves behind. They were handed large offices and important-sounding job titles and Filipina housemaids and a sense of grandeur that I suspect many of them always knew, deep down, was little more than the formal dressing of life in a petrostate. And just as they (and we, and most everyone who comes to places like Qatar to do anything other than manual labor) became bigger, in Montreal my family settled into our smaller selves. My father's work credentials meant nothing here, he struggled to find a job. There were of course other routine indignities—people instinctively speaking louder and slower once they heard my parents' accents, the kids at my high school who asked if everyone got around by camel where I came from—but these you learn to flatten into the normal workings of the day, the price of admission. The smallness, though, it warps the bones.

The first years in Montreal are not good ones. On my days off from school I hover around downtown: Sainte-Catherine Street, the pubs and the deps and the heat-lamp dives where drunk American teenagers—not yet old enough to buy alcohol back home—go to gorge themselves on poutine. I wander around the college campuses. There's always a kind of anonymity available to any young person who wanders around a college campus. My high school has an arrangement with Concordia University that allows us to borrow books from the university library. I spend months working up the courage to go in there and make use of it.

One night, I go to a party at the home of an old friend from Qatar who had been sent to Montreal by his father ostensibly to continue his education but instead has made quite a decent living for himself selling crack. One of the people there, aggressively enthusiastic in that way only certain men between the ages of seventeen and twenty-two become when they first stumble onto the work of William Burroughs, says to me with complete conviction that *Naked Lunch* is the finest novel ever written, and that I know nothing of life until I read it. There's a man in that book who's being consumed by his own asshole, the young man says to me, very seriously, do you understand? Do you understand the *meaning*? I nod. The next morning, I go to the Concordia library.

I remember a sense of fear, real fear, as I half-whisper the name of this book to the librarian at the desk. In another life I'd once smuggled a copy of Dennis Rodman's biography—the one with a picture of his bare ass on the back cover—to Qatar from a summer trip in Florida. Back in the old country you got deported for reading the wrong thing, watching the wrong thing, thinking the wrong thing.

Completely disinterested, the librarian points me in the direction of a row in the stacks. I pick the book off the shelves, whisk it home, read it in one sitting, don't understand a word. It's exhilarating.

The overwhelming ordinariness of that day, and yet how it marked a small parcel of rootedness in those years when the West transformed from a thing on film and television to the place where, more likely than not, I'd live out the rest of my life. I remember thinking: If this is all there is, it's enough. Maybe you don't ever shake off the mangling of your name or the dumb jokes about camels, but at least you go to the library and you read whatever you choose. You go to the movies and *Titanic* isn't ninety minutes long and seemingly edited by a prudish maniac.

I knew none of this was for my benefit, but I could make a home within it. I believed, firmly, not in any ceiling on what this society would allow to be done to people like me, but in what it would allow done to itself, its own rights and freedoms and principles.

And that was fine, that was plenty. It anchored me through those early, alien years. Anchored me later, too, when I lucked into the only real job I've ever had: journalism—a profession where, daily and in the most unpredictable ways, such beliefs are tested.

●

Our training began with a fake ambush. There were about a dozen of us in the SUVs, headed from the hotel to some anonymous parcel of farmland in rural Virginia. Our instructors, a bunch of former special ops troops who had found a lucrative second career in private security and what is often called "hazardous environment training," told us nothing about what was to come that first day. Afterward, they asked us not to tell anyone else, which makes this anecdote a bit of a betrayal. At the end of an unpaved, single-lane road that snaked through the pines, we came to a metal gate. The cars stopped, and as our driver made to open the door, a bunch of armed, masked men stormed the car from behind the trees. Shouting and pointing their weapons at our heads, they dragged us out of the vehicles, bound our hands, covered our faces in thick black cloth, and marched us through the forest. We were made to get down on our knees. Gunfire echoed in the near distance. After a few minutes of this, each of us was pulled up and taken to a clearing, where the cloth was lifted from our heads and, as the world came back into focus, we saw a man holding a camcorder to our faces. In a little while, we would be shown the footage—our instructors wanted us to see the looks on our faces, which on this day ranged from sobbing to bemusement.

(We were told that, in the previous session, a man had broken down completely when the hood came off. At first, the instructors thought he suffered from some prior trauma, that he had been through something awful, and this exercise had brought it all back. Turns out they weren't completely wrong: he had had a bad experience at an S&M club that also involved a hood and handcuffs. He was a musician, and had decided to attend hazardous environment training because he wanted to fly to Iraq and write a rock opera about the U.S. invasion. I think about this man at least once a month.)

It is the case, for most major news organizations, that no journalist can be sent into a war zone or other destabilized corner of the world without this kind of training—the insurance companies would balk. For a week, we spent our days on the farm, learning from men who had lived part of their lives in the faraway arena of great industrial violence. We were taught the basics of combat first aid (tie a tourniquet around it and get the hell out of there). We were told to always bribe as close to the going rate as possible, never more, so as to not contribute to inflation. One particular exercise involved having us close our eyes and mentally estimate the passing of one minute, then raise our hands. The first hand came up at around thirty seconds, the last around three minutes. We were then asked to close our eyes once more and walk in a straight line for one hundred meters. Within a few minutes, there were people wandering all over the field, in every direction. One person had to be wrangled before they wandered into a nearby forest. Finally, we were brought back and taught the undeniable lesson of the exercise: left to their own devices, most human beings are useless at estimating time, distance, or space.

That same day, in a classroom session on war zone preparedness, one of the instructors told us to think about what he called a "rape plan." There might come a time, he said, when two colleagues find themselves in a situation where one is subjected to something terrible and the other can do nothing about it. To not think through this ahead of time—the worst possible thing, and the aftermath—is a mistake, he said. There's no coming back from a situation where one person believes a particular response on the other's behalf, and that response doesn't come. For a week, this was the nature of instruction: these men trying, as gently as the circumstances demanded, to get a group of war-novice reporters to understand what it feels like when the rules of the reasonable world melt away.

It was the middle of 2007, shortly before my first short stint covering the NATO invasion of Afghanistan. I was working as a journalist at *The Globe and Mail*, which bills itself as Canada's national newspaper and, although the folks at the *Toronto Star* and the *National Post* might tell you otherwise, is pretty well the country's newspaper of record. I was twenty-five years old and for months I had been pestering the *Globe*'s foreign editor to give me an assignment, any assignment. I wanted desperately to be in the world, telling stories of consequence—stories that, had you not read about them in my articles, you wouldn't have read at all. This seemed to me then, and still does now, the only kind of journalism any journalist should want to do. Everything else, to paraphrase the common saying about meetings and emails, could have been a press release.

Six years earlier, on a Tuesday in early September, I woke up in my basement apartment in Kingston, Ontario, and realized that I had slept in—not so flagrantly as to make it impossible for me to get to my first college class of the school year on time, but enough that I didn't really want to. I was an aimless sophomore at Queen's University and, over the course of the next few years, I would attend barely enough classes to count on two hands. I had no idea what I was doing with my life. The only thing I had ever wanted to do was write. I also knew, as I suspect many children of immigrants in the West do, that you don't write for a living; you don't paint, you don't sing—you become an engineer, a lawyer, a doctor. Such were the familial and cultural mechanics that landed me in an undergrad computer science program that, to this day, I find it utterly baffling I left with a degree of any kind.

Skipping class now a foregone conclusion, I got up. I checked my email. The first message was from a high school friend who had gone on to study at Columbia.

hi, everyone,

i just thought i'd write a quick note to let everyone know
i'm ok. i'm very far from the center of this tragedy, like you

guys, so far i've only seen it on t.v. it's a complete shock,
as it is to everyone, i'm sure. outside, you can hear sirens
blaring, and it's hard to describe how it feels to know that a
few miles away, a terrorist act has occurred.

I got up, went to the living room, turned on the television, saw footage of the second plane hitting the building.

A few weeks after the 9/11 attacks, I joined the staff of the college newspaper. I had no idea how a newspaper worked, only that something had changed, the world had changed, and I wanted to write about it. My first published story was about a group of students who'd started a fundraiser for the victims of the attacks. Four years later, armed with a middling portfolio of features and short news hits, I was offered a summer internship at the *Globe*'s head office in Toronto. It was there, over the next ten years, that I received an education—in writing, in reporting, in the mechanics of the world.

■

In a report from one of the towns Hamas fighters attacked on October 7, an Israeli journalist mentions news of slaughtered infants. There's no shortage of atrocities, documented atrocities, to report on, but it is this story that, unsurprisingly, provokes the most shock. It becomes, in the days that follow, something even more gruesome: forty beheaded babies. Myriad media outlets in the West run with it. In the weeks to come, virtually no correspondents from these outlets will be able to see what happens inside Gaza. They will instead report from hotel room balconies in Tel Aviv or go on guided tours with the same military whose own killing spree they are prohibited from covering firsthand. But this story, of beheaded babies, will in the early days of the genocide come to define an essential unburdening. Almost a quarter century earlier, reports of phantom uranium helped garner support for a war that killed upward of a million people. Now, once more, an essential truth of calamity journalism is made clear: In the earliest days, in the chaos that precedes systemic annihilation, it is not what the party deemed most malicious has actually done that matters, but rather what it is believed capable of doing.

About midway through my time at *The Globe and Mail*, the union got into a contract dispute with management. These things happen all the time, especially in an industry as perpetually cash-strapped as print journalism. We were urged by our union reps to make sure we had personal email accounts, in case our work ones were cut off. There was some talk of designing and distributing our own publication in the case of a lockout.

Of all the sticking points in the new contract, perhaps the stickiest had to do with branded content. Different media outlets have different names for this sort of thing, but it usually entails allowing companies to run covert ads in the form of articles. Maybe Toyota has a new line of SUVs coming out, and simply gobbling up the bottom-right quarter of page A2 isn't giving them enough bang for their buck. So instead, the company approaches a newspaper and pays for a special supplement on the SUV revolution: articles that read like traditional news stories, but would not exist had the advertiser not paid for them. Can management force reporters to take on such assignments, treat them no different than real news? The two sides of the bargaining table had very different opinions on the matter.

At the time, the reporters were livid. Today, after countless rounds of layoffs and the prospect of AI-generated noise coming to replace human-written stories of any kind, it almost seems quaint.

Journalists are human. They have mortgages and bills. They work jobs so precarious, demanding, and poorly paying that about half the cohort of reporters I began my career with now work in public relations. There's a reason journalism boasts one of the highest divorce rates of any industry. You work weird hours. You get yelled at a lot. You're asked to write five listicles a day for the web traffic. You're asked to do a professional videographer's job on the side, with your iPhone. Your mistakes are a matter of public record, forever.

It's not particularly difficult to see the aftereffects of these forces, especially the economic ones. The most glaring example in the Western world is Fox News, an entity that more than any other has normalized the practice of severing any relationship between the truth and what one wishes the truth to be. It's a common refrain that the news industry has failed to come up with a functioning business model in the Internet age, but that's not entirely true. Jettisoning the requirement to report news in favor of inciting the rage and fear and hatred of your audience before serving them up ads for guns and bunkers is a perfectly functional business model. It might not be journalism, might be the opposite of journalism, but the checks clear.

They say what you're supposed to do, in this line of work, is comfort the afflicted and afflict the comfortable. I heard that saying a lot, as a young journalist. Believed in it, too. It's a quote originally from a piece of fiction, spoken by a character who can't stand the press.

There's always been a contradiction at the heart of this enterprise. In the modern, well-dressed definition, adhered to in one form or another at almost every major newspaper, the journalist cannot be an activist, must remain allegiant to a self-erasing neutrality. Yet journalism at its core is one of the most activist endeavors there is. A reporter is supposed to agitate against power, against privilege. Against the slimy wall of press releases and PR nothingspeak that has come to protect every major business and government boardroom ever since Watergate. A reporter is supposed to agitate against silence.

To maintain both these realities at the same time—of the neutral agitator—requires a cognitive dissonance that can be seen in every corner of the industry. In much of the world, the most prestigious journalism prizes honor public service, which is to say stories that prompt institutional change, send a corrupt mayor to jail, or force the ending of an unjust policy. But journalists themselves cannot call for justice.

Except when they can. More than a few of my former colleagues, in the aftermath of the Russian invasion of Ukraine and the Hamas attacks on Israel, proudly boasted of their support for both Ukraine and Israel. When Russian authorities detained and eventually convicted *Wall Street Journal* reporter Evan Gershkovich in an obvious sham of a judicial process, almost every Western media outlet called it what it was.

But as the Israeli military wiped out both Palestinian journalists and their entire families in a deliberate campaign to silence the flow of information out of Gaza, virtually all the same colleagues, all the same outlets, took a very different approach. The profession of journalism necessitates a capacity to understand things, and all who watched the killings understood what was happening.

There's a model of self-perception among some journalists that views the world as a playing field and the reporter as some combination of referee, scorekeeper, and play-by-play announcer. It's a model that seeks to assign agency while maintaining the veneer of both neutrality and objectivity. If there's a foul, the referee will call it, regardless of which team is responsible. The announcer will tell you what happened. The scorekeeper will tell you the results. No favor, no bias. One can see the consequences of this kind of model most frequently in political coverage, where the chief concern of so many stories is not the substance of the policy proposal but the way it moves the polls. It's a bizarre, destructive form of pragmatism—the jettisoning of moral faculties in favor of a near-Machiavellian view of the world.

But it is also symbiotic, as vital to the people being reported on as it is to the people doing the reporting. I remember, early in the 2016 election campaign, Donald Trump musing about forcing American Muslims to carry special identification cards—a proposal that is by any honest measure reminiscent of the preamble to some of history's worst atrocities. Hillary Clinton condemned the idea and returned to her talking point about how American Muslims were important allies in the War on Terror, the government's "eyes and ears" on the front lines of radicalization and extremism.

That's not why such a proposal deserves condemnation. It deserves condemnation because it is morally repugnant. But morals complicate the matter. They introduce an obligation to oppose. They also force everyone involved to confront the fact that a significant swath of the American electorate does indeed consider the affected group to be so threatening, so inherently barbaric, that making them carry special identification cards becomes perfectly acceptable. And that, in turn, forces a reckoning with what the United States has become, or has always been. So instead, the coverage shifts to a flattened mode, listing claim and counterclaim, measuring the impact on the poll numbers. Everything becomes a horse race.

How long a society can function under such a journalistic model before deteriorating into something unsalvageable is an open question. But the entire notion of reporter as referee/ announcer/scorekeeper, even if it has any merit, requires the game on the field to be played in accordance with some set of rules. It has no capacity to deal with players who kneecap their opponents in the locker room, who have no interest in the rules or even the game itself. Listing one position and then the other and letting the reader make up their own mind fails entirely in the face of plain bad faith. The result is absurdity: articles in which the reporter has had to pretzel their way to a level playing field between the claim that fewer guns would reduce gun violence and the claim that more guns will reduce gun violence. Neatly wrapped-up paragraphs of what in the industry is called "M-copy," explaining the background of a conflict by listing an act of aggression by one party and then an offsetting one by the other, absent historical context, so as not to be seen as taking sides. A deranged Republican talking point presented with at best mild rebuke because there are only two major political parties in America and one of them just happens to be populated with the sort of people who muse about whether wildfires are caused by Jewish space lasers.

But this is centrism. This is the high-minded middle ground. The only serious, nuanced position, in such circles, is to plant oneself firmly halfway between what is assumed to be the standard left and standard right. Should one party propose stripping immigrants of all rights and the other propose stripping them of only some rights, the intellectually rigorous thing to do is to consider that what's best is stripping immigrants of most rights. To compromise.

Good journalism should have no interest in any of this. And there is plenty of exceptional journalism in the world, despite the industry's countless failings. As I write this, Palestinian reporters are in effect the world's sole source of information about the reality of the obliteration of Gaza, the plain truth of the horror in the face of a mass propagandist effort that at

43

one point included the president of the United States claiming to have seen pictures of dead babies he never saw, claiming a United States ally did not bomb a hospital among the myriad hospitals it now regularly bombs. The price of reporting under these conditions is everything. As of July 2024, at least 108 Palestinian journalists have been killed, according to the Committee to Protect Journalists. There is nowhere else on earth with an even remotely comparable death toll. For the crime of reporting in a way the Israeli government disapproves of, Al Jazeera correspondent Wael Dahdouh sees his family summarily executed in a missile strike. He continues reporting the next day. Shortly thereafter he himself is wounded. He continues reporting the next day. That most every major Western journalism prize that emerges from the coverage of this onslaught will overlook or at best offer glancing recognition of the work of men and women like Dahdouh for fear of being labeled biased is as clear an indictment of the industry's cracked moral compass as exists anywhere.

The most frustrating aspect of all this is that most journalists know how to be tenacious. They know how to chase down a story, how to speak truth to power. In articles about atrocities committed by groups or nations that are not Western allies, nobody ever perishes in a blast. Buildings don't collapse of their own volition. Civilian victims aren't ordered by their interviewers to performatively condemn groups with which they have no affiliation. The violence is named, as is its perpetrator. Why this sudden clarity becomes utter fog when the subject is an Arab child torn to shreds by shrapnel or a

Black motorist shot dead in a traffic stop or an Indigenous activist beaten at a pipeline protest is a function of preemptive deference to power. Some people can't do much more than write a letter to the editor. Some have the ability to pull advertising, to limit access. Most insidiously, some have the power to berate the people who run those media outlets when they next meet at a cocktail party or black-tie fundraiser or whatever social circle in which both move. I'm sure it's not the case that every editor of every major publication in the West doesn't give a damn about all those inconvenient Brown people who keep getting killed and maimed by the thousands. But to never see these people in daily life, to never converse with them outside the bounds of interrogation, to never have reason to consider them human in any social sense—these things bleed into the story, or the absence of story. The afflicted don't need comforting, they need what the comfortable have always had.

On a day in late December 2023, as the killing in Gaza nears its third month, U.S. Secretary of State Antony Blinken posts a short missive on social media lamenting what a deadly year it has been for journalists around the world, and noting how sad it is that reporters can be killed for simply doing their jobs. It is, of course, pablum, utterly meaningless and of a particularly amoral quality given the U.S. government's unwavering support of Israel, the nation responsible for killing more of those journalists than any other. Blinken knows this, knows that a significant part of his job involves parroting ethical stances in the abstract that his own administration actively undermines in reality. I understand this is just how things are, ethical double-jointedness being a necessary requirement for the daily debasements of modern political life. And yet I still wonder how someone can maintain this particular facade and sleep at night. The journalists who bring the reality of the world to light are daily slaughtered. Meanwhile, an embarrassing number of their Western colleagues, who for the most part fear no such outcome but accept it as the sad lot of those distant others, travel within the protective cocoon of people like the very concerned secretary and measure his vacuous declarations of solidarity with their craft as just another part of the horse race, just another part of the game.

CHAPTER THREE

VALUES

A woman's leg amputated, without anesthesia, the surgery conducted on a kitchen table. A boy holding his father's shoe, screaming. A girl whose jaw has been torn off. A child, still in diapers, pulled out of the tents after the firebombing, his head severed from his body.

Is there distance great enough, to be free of this? To be made clean?

Abbotsford, 2000:

My father shrugs at us as the officer eases his head into the back of the police cruiser. I remember, clearly, his face as he looks at us through the rear-seat window and mouths the words, It's going to be OK. I remember it like it was yesterday, though I know it's not true, simply something I invented after the fact. He would have never used those words, would have never used English. Not then, not to us. If he said anything, it would have been, *M'tkhafoosh, ma feesh mashakel.* English was for the officers.

There's a village in the forests of southern British Columbia, about ninety minutes east of Vancouver, called Harrison Hot Springs. It's beautiful, curled up around the lake, the sort of place people get away to for the long weekends and the holidays, all golf courses and mineral pools. After a year without work in Montreal, my father finally finds a job at a hotel in Harrison. The first time I go out to visit him, I stand at the shore of the lake and look out at the low squat hills. I know right away there's nothing here for my father besides a paycheck. I know he's already looking for another elsewhere, another leaving. Years later it dawns on me that the immigrant class, which in one form or another describes (or will come to describe, in the looming, cataclysmic decades of the Anthropocene) most of the world, is segregated by many things, chief among them narrative. Some are afforded the privilege of an arrival story, a homecoming. Others, only departure after departure.

A few days in Harrison and we're climbing the walls. One can only sit in a hot spring for so long. On a whim, my father decides we should drive the twenty hours south to visit my mother's uncle Mohammed in Los Angeles. They had been best friends since childhood, the two Mohammeds, and the few times we'd gone to visit in the past, they seemed to exist within the confines of a shorthand only available to old friends, similarly uprooted. The shorthand of people who were familiar with more than just each other's multiple leavings. Who'd also shared arrivals.

At the Abbotsford crossing, which runs along the border

between British Columbia and Washington, an American guard flips through our passports as though there's something mildly offensive slathered on the pages, something he'll have to wash off later. We experience the stillness of time passing: those few seconds, sometimes minutes, sometimes hours, where like a thrown ball suspended at the apex, you wait. You wait on gravity, a movement predetermined but yet to come.

Pull into that spot over there, the guard says.

At secondary, we watch a small group of officers consult one another quietly. They pass our passports back and forth. A few years later, at a checkpoint near Marfa, Texas, where the guard takes one look at my face and assumes I'm Mexican, I'd experience that same sense of prolonged suspension, of waiting on judgment. By then I'd gotten Canadian citizenship, and anyway we were nowhere near a border, just pulled over at a checkpoint within that obscenely large space the U.S. government considers border territory. (There's a small subgenre of videos on the Internet in which people—almost without fail white American men—film themselves refusing to comply at these non–border crossings. The phrase "I know my rights" comes up a lot.) I'd be told to pull over, and for a half hour I'd wait and occasionally watch one of the guards do the exact same thing I used to do as a child with all those censored magazines back in Qatar. He'd hold my passport up to the light, looking for something hidden.

In Abbotsford, too, a guard holds our passports to the light, runs his finger along the text inside. Eventually, he comes over to where my parents and I sit. He tells us we'd been denied

49

entry. My mother and I are ushered back to the car, but my father is handed over to the Canadians. An officer puts him in the back of a police cruiser. He is taken to a nearby police station. My mother and I are told to go home.

Hours later, we get the call to come pick him up. The ordinary indignity of it: I remember being angry—angry in a very specific way that, until that moment, I felt myself immune to by virtue of my flawless English accent, my cultural fluency, my ability to pass. Angry is something foreigners got. Not people like me, not people who'd put in the work.

(Once, I went to visit an acquaintance in Europe who had immigrated from the Arab world with her family as a very young child. She had become fluent in the language, the culture—by all accounts, had assimilated. One night, while she was giving me a walking tour of the city, a BMW raced by, windows open, Arabic music blasting. She shook her head. Damn Arabs, she said.)

There was never much of an explanation as to why we were denied entry that day in Abbotsford. Maybe it was my father's shadowy terrorist namesake again. Maybe it was because a few months earlier a man named Ahmed Ressam had tried to cross into Port Angeles with a hundred pounds of explosives, and so the guards could be forgiven for their extra caution around another Arab man. And anyway, it wasn't our country, we weren't owed entry. Maybe it was just bad luck.

If it bothers him, my father doesn't show it. Of all his personality traits, I think the central one was a belief that the more rational, reasoned argument should always win.

In his youth, he had wanted to study pure mathematics; he moved through arguments as a mathematician moves through proofs—stepwise: *So therefore . . .*

On the car ride home from the police station, he seems quite proud that the Canadian officers were baffled as to why their American counterparts had asked he be taken in and investigated.

The following year, in 2001, my father receives a job offer in Wisconsin. It's a good job. It pays well and the hotel where he'd work is in a city several times bigger than Harrison Hot Springs. The only logistical hurdle is a work visa, which his prospective employer tells him won't be an issue, they do this sort of thing all the time. Then September 11 comes.

Suddenly the application stalls. For months and months everyone waits. Finally, the hotel manager has to find someone else for the job. There's the same vague undercurrent of pride in my father's voice as he tells me what happened, how apologetic the manager sounded. A wrong had been done but at least everyone acknowledged it was not rational.

Again I'm angry and again I understand my anger is worthless. In the West whose stories I had grown up consuming, so much depended on the cleansing power of righteous anger. And it occurs to me then, maybe for the first time in my life, that when Rambo leveled that small Washington town, or when Hunter S. Thompson made the cop chase him for miles along the desert highway just for the hell of it, it was never just an expression of ballsiness or rebellion or righteous anything. What the men who'd lived or dreamed up these stories understood was that the plausibility of such transgression depended on who the system being rebelled against was made to serve. Narrative power, maybe all power, was never about flaunting the rules, yelling at a cop, making trouble—it was about knowing that, for a privileged class, there existed a hard ceiling on the consequences.

And on the heels of that realization, a converse one: I begin to suspect that the principles holding up this place might not withstand as much as I first thought. That the entire edifice of equality under law and process, of fair treatment, could just as easily be set aside to reward those who belong as to punish those who don't. A hard ceiling for some, no floor for others.

●

I watch footage of people bringing their kids to a party of sorts. Only it's not a party, it's a blockade. The people are here to stop aid trucks from entering Gaza. But the atmosphere is festive. Someone on the other side of these walls is going to starve to death or be operated on without proper medical equipment because this aid won't pass, but there is something festive here. Ten years earlier, when I watch footage of settlers with folding chairs up on the hillside, viewing the bombing of Gaza as one would view a summer blockbuster, again there is a celebratory air. I am reminded of what the actor Helen Mirren said of her time in Israel in 1967: "I saw Arabs being thrown out of their houses in Jerusalem. But it was just the extraordinary magical energy of a country just beginning to put its roots in the ground. It was an amazing time to be here."

And then I watch former vice president Mike Pence write messages of support on the side of bombs.

He smiles as he does this, as he commits his name and whatever exists of his conscience to the machinery of wholesale murder. The people around him smile. They take pictures. Again, there is about the grotesquerie a current of catharsis, a lightness akin to the freeing of a pants button after a heavy meal, making peace with insatiable appetite.

As always, the dead will be made to pay the moral debt born of their killing. At the start of this campaign, one oft-parroted justification was the nonsensical contrivance that Palestinians in Gaza were subject to a collective guilt on account of their voting for Hamas. It is somewhat pointless to note that most Gazans are too young to have voted for Hamas in the most recent election, or that collective punishment of a civilian population for their electoral choices would be subject to a far higher standard of scrutiny if that population weren't a politically powerless contingent of Brown people, or that the very same terror group had long received support from the Israeli government as a matter of strategy so as to keep an entity in power that at least partially shared the government's disdain for peace or a two-state solution, or that the occupation and terror inflicted on Palestinians long predates the creation of Hamas. It is pointless, even, to make the obvious analogies, to imagine the response had almost any other country on earth killed hundreds or thousands of civilians on a hostage rescue mission, or flattened every hospital in a city on the hunt for a terror group, and then bragged about its success. Pointless because such things assume a conversation anchored in facts or reason or even the thinnest presupposition that the people being killed, like those killed on October 7, are human beings, their loss an utter indictment of the systems and leaders and world that allowed it. Instead, as the scope and scale of annihilation intensifies, an opposite presupposition becomes necessary, one that imposes onto the dead the appropriate mendacity to justify their killing. A few weeks in, the notion that Palestinians deserve to die because some of them voted for Hamas becomes insufficient to hold up the body count. Soon, Palestinians become indistinguishable from Nazis, and then worse than Nazis. As their eradication continues, they must transform into the worst human beings on earth, the weight of their deaths only then sufficiently lightened.

Everyone involved—the dead, their killers, the arbiters of the exchange rate—knows this for what it is. In 2014, when an Israeli newspaper runs an opinion piece in which the writer describes Palestinian children as "the explosives of the future," there's no ambiguity as to what is happening, what is desired to happen. Seven months before the Hamas attacks of October 2023, when the same newspaper publishes and then quickly deletes a post titled "When Genocide Is Permissible," the bedrock of polite intellectual discourse that liberalism so desperately and invariably sees as a hallmark of its own enlightenment is shown to be a phantom thing—a premise that, when most needed, cedes the floor to the concrete vocabulary of violence. And then following the attacks, when Israeli defense minister Yoav Gallant says Israel is fighting "human animals," it is not a statement of belief so much as permission. When those dying are deemed human enough to warrant discussion, discussion must be had. When they're deemed nonhuman, discussion becomes offensive, an affront to civility.

What power assumes, ultimately, is that all those who weren't directly affected by this, who only had to bear the minor inconvenience of hearing about these deaths from afar, will move on, will forget. Tomorrow more Palestinians will die, but in the places where the bombs are built and launched it will have no bearing on mortgages, bills, employment. Indeed, in many of these places, what will have a real economic effect is if the bombing *stops*. In social and professional circles there will be limited tolerance for any talk about the fortunes of some exotic, dangerous-sounding people. In the context of self-interest—and maybe there never was any other context—it is utter madness to risk one's own prospects standing up for people who can offer nothing in return. Tomorrow more Palestinians will die, but the unsaid thing is that it is all right because that's what those people do, they die. *Just for a moment, cease to believe that this particular group of people are human.*

For millions of Westerners this will always prove true.

But for millions more it will not. In moments such as these, when the lies are so glaring and the bodies so many, millions will come to understand that there is no such thing as "those people." Instinctively this will be known to those who have seen it before, who have seen their land or labor stolen, their people killed, and know the voracity of violent taking. Those who learned not to forget the Latin American death squads, the Vietnamese and Cambodian and Laotian villages turned to ash, the Congolese rubber then and Congolese coltan now, the nice clean beach an hour north of Tel Aviv that sits atop a mass grave.

But even the most sheltered will at least be given reason to reconsider what any system capable of justifying such things can do. When a man signs his name to a bomb and smiles, who that bomb is used to kill isn't even an afterthought. It can't be.

And yet there is a deranged honesty about the cult to which the likes of Pence—and former South Carolina governor Nikki Haley, who signed her own message, "Finish them!," to similar bombs—belong. American liberalism demands a rhetorical politeness from which the fascistic iteration of the modern Republican Party is fully free. There is something stomach-churning about watching a parade of Biden administration press secretaries offer insincere expressions of concern for Palestinians as the same administration bankrolls their butcher. It is a reminder that the Democratic Party's relationship with progressivism so often ends at the lawn sign: Proclaim support for this minority group or that. Hang a rainbow flag one month a year from some White House window. Most important, remind everyone at every turn of how much worse the alternative would be.

Against such hollow gesturing, even the most unhinged Republican will always be able to say: Look, these people have no interest in your suffering, only in empty gestures; I'll do away with gestures, and make the right people suffer. It is an astoundingly effective technique, but would not be if the leadership of the Democratic Party had come to realize that sloganeering without concrete action means nothing.

When it matters, everyone recognizes meaningless pageantry. Amid one of the largest killing sprees of Muslims in recent history, amid a wave of hate attacks that sees a six-year-old boy murdered in his Chicago home by a man rabid with loathing for anyone remotely Middle Eastern, the Biden administration happily announces the creation of a task force on Islamophobia. (Without looking it up, can you recall a single thing this task force has done? Does it still exist?) When a growing number of staffers begin to publicly bristle about their boss's support for mass killing, the White House's solution is to throw a morale-boosting party. It is a reminder that, in times like these, one remarkable difference between the modern Western conservative and their liberal counterpart is that the former will gleefully sign their name on the side of the bomb while the latter will just sheepishly initial it.

As has become custom these past twenty years, a predictable chorus of voices reemerges to remind American Muslims, Arabs, minorities of all kinds—and really anyone who would normally be a reliable blue vote—not to waver in their support.

Don't let the Biden administration's endorsement of mass murder distract from the reality that a Trump administration would be so much worse. That this campaign tactic reemerges every election cycle is a testament to its effectiveness. It is not quite accurate to say the Republican Party is more destructive on virtually every domestic and foreign policy issue, because such a statement would imply that the party has any interest in policy as it exists in normal, civil society.

After chiding activists who warned years ago of the Republican Party's descent into outright fascism, mainstream Democrats have now fully embraced the accusation. It's become difficult to find a single Democratic campaign appeal that doesn't lean hard on the warning that the Trump wing of the GOP—which is now the only viable wing of the GOP—represents an existential threat to democracy, the United States itself.

Fight it, then. Propose something to meet the nature of the moment. It can't be the case both that the Supreme Court is an unaccountable neoconservative body intent on rendering the whole country unrecognizable and that there's simply no way to do anything significant about it. It can't be that climate change is the single most important issue facing the world, with our entire species at risk, and drilling licenses need to continue. It can't be that innocent Palestinians have faced unbearable suffering and we care very deeply about their plight, and absolutely nothing will stop the arming of the nation responsible. It can't be both rhetorical urgency and policymaking impotence.

—

Of course the Republicans would be worse. What the mainstream Democrat seems incapable of accepting is that, for an even remotely functioning conscience, there exists a point beyond which relative harm can no longer offset absolute evil. For a lot of people, genocide is that point. Suddenly, an otherwise very persuasive argument takes on a different meaning: "Vote for the liberal though he harms you because the conservative will harm you more" starts to sound a lot like "Vote for the liberal though he harms you because the conservative might harm me, too."

In reality, not a single Western politician or party, not a single government anywhere in the world, can be expected to change when constantly rewarded this way. The argument in favor of voting for the lesser evil is frequently made in good faith, by people who have plenty to lose should the greater evil win. But it also establishes the lowest of benchmarks: *Want my vote? Be less monstrous than the monsters.*

But to say this—that mainstream liberal parties will never develop a moral compass until they are punished for not having one—produces a level of antagonistic vitriol unmatched in almost any other context. Waves of progressives will take time out from pasting MY RELIGION IS LOVE stickers to the bumpers of their Teslas to let you know that advocating this position makes you the enemy, that they hope you're happy when Trump takes power and makes your life even more miserable, that you should just go back to where you came from.

(It's a fascinating directive, *Go back to where you came from.* One can't help but wonder how changed the world would be had the ancestors of the same people who use that phrase now heeded the same advice then. Overwhelmingly, it's employed against anyone who tries to make use of the freedoms on which the West so prides itself: the freedom to speak and to criticize, to hold power accountable. In this way, it shares a deep bond with the approach to free expression that can be found in most dictatorships and authoritarian regimes, the places so many immigrants fled: You are free to say so long as what you say is acceptable. Whenever I am told to go back to where I came from, I can't help but think: Why don't *you* go where I came from? You'd love it there.)

I watch a speech in South Carolina where Joe Biden is interrupted by protesters, one of whom shouts, "Twenty thousand dead Palestinians, their blood is on your hands." Some of Biden's supporters try to drown this out with chants of "Four more years, four more years."

Earlier the same day, demonstrators shut down the bridges into Manhattan. As with all such acts of disobedience, the usual cavalry of talking heads emerges to note that these protests only inconvenience people, and that inconveniencing people is not an effective way to change their minds. Never is this logic applied to the past, to the demonstrations that shut down bridges to call for an end to segregation, for example. Because if applied to a moment already deemed righteous in hindsight, such an argument would be shown immediately for its spinelessness. But for now, it's fine. For now, a motorist made late for work or a colonizer's portrait disfigured provokes more of a political response than any number of dead foreign kids can.

Before the one-year anniversary of the October 7 murders and the genocide in Gaza, the Conservatives are out in the United Kingdom, replaced by Labour in a landslide. In France, what seemed like a certain victory for the far right instead ends up a victory for a center-left coalition. In the United States, a Democratic president whose support for Israel's obliteration of Gaza cost him massive swaths of the progressive and youth votes, but who ultimately lost all hope when his own political and donor circles abandoned him, announces he is not running for reelection. In so many of the most powerful nations on earth, utter fascists either maintain immense power or threaten to snatch it. But as much as the mainstream liberal parties might be far less deranged and cruel than their right-wing opponents on virtually every policy issue, it is the case of Palestinian suffering—or more precisely, utter indifference to it—where the two sides seem to be most in agreement.

What ensures it won't be this way forever? Either hundreds of millions of people have always been predisposed to the lure of the fascist, in which case the entire democratic endeavor is doomed anyway, or something of corporate liberalism has brought us here. Whatever the quality of its rhetoric, any politics that buckles at the prospect of even mildly inconveniencing the rich, or resisting an ally's genocidal intentions, will always face an uphill battle against a politics that actively embraces malice. "Yes We Can" is a conditional. "Yes We Will" is not.

The moral component of history, the most necessary component, is simply a single question, asked over and over again: When it mattered, who sided with justice and who sided with power? What makes moments such as this one so dangerous, so clarifying, is that one way or another everyone is forced to answer.

CHAPTER FOUR

LANGUAGE

When the past is past, the dead will be found to not have partaken in their own killing. The families huddled in the corridors of the hospital will not have tied their hands behind their backs, lined themselves against the wall, shot themselves in the heads, and then hopped into mass graves of their own volition. The prisoners in the torture camps will not have penetrated themselves with electric rods. The children will not have pulled their own limbs out and strewn them all over the makeshift soccer pitch. The babies will not have chosen starvation.

When the past is past. But for now, who's to say they didn't? Who can truly be sure, but the killers and the dead?

Forward Operating Base Masum Ghar, 2007:

There's a ragged wound in the side of the shower tent where the shrapnel had come through. Bullets, by comparison, make clean entry. Shrapnel rends. Near the entrance to the base, someone puts the zeros back up on the PROUD TO BE ROCKET

FREE FOR ___ DAYS sign. It hasn't gone up past one in a month, a soldier says to me.

In the fall of 2007, at the age of twenty-five, after pestering the foreign editor for months, I'm put on the Afghanistan rotation, my first assignment covering war. It's a temporary thing, filling in for our regular correspondent. These are the middle days of the NATO invasion, and many Western media outlets still feel the need to have at least a semipermanent presence in the country. I'm ecstatic. It's impossible to do the work of journalism, or at least serious journalism, and not be forced to make some kind of peace with the reality that you will be, many times over, a tourist in someone else's misery. You will drop into the lives of people suffering the worst things human beings can do to one another. And no matter how empathetic or sincere or even apologetic for your privilege you may be, when you are done you will exercise the privilege of leaving. Some reporters learn to make peace with it, justify it (*How else will the public know what's happening here? How else will change come about?*). My first time out, I ignore it entirely. I'm young: this will be an adventure, a grand adventure.

I arrive at the sprawling NATO airfield in Kandahar. It's a small city of tents and repurposed shipping containers that boasts its own Burger King. Once, during my stay there, the Dallas Cowboys cheerleaders are flown in and give a performance creepily reminiscent of the scene in *Apocalypse Now*. After a few days, I hitch a ride with a convoy of Canadian soldiers headed to the forward operating bases. The morning we are set to leave, I climb into the back of a light armored vehicle, one of four that make up the convoy. LAVs are usually built with upward-arched chassis, so as to dissipate the impact of a landmine or improvised explosive device. On arrival at the airfield, most everyone is briefed, at length and with much use of acronyms, about various kinds of IEDs—VBIEDs (vehicle-borne), PBIEDs (person-borne? personnel-borne? I forget), DBIEDs (donkey-borne). Occasionally, the reporters argue about which LAV in the four-vehicle formation is, on average, the safest to ride in. You want to be in the lead, one reporter tells me, because a lot of the time the explosives don't go off until after the first one crosses, and anyway you don't want to be pinned behind a vehicle that can't move. I have no idea if there's any truth to it, but he seems confident. The worst and most successful war reporters I meet are all very confident.

The convoy arrives at Forward Operating Base Masum Ghar in the afternoon. The FOBs, relatively tiny and for the most part scattered in remote locations, tend to be much less well protected than the major bases. Masum Ghar, a cliffside outpost about an hour west of the city of Kandahar, had come under rocket-propelled grenade fire almost every night for a month straight by the time we get there. They are not sophisticated attacks: most times, it's only a man approaching in the middle of the night, armed with something the Soviets left behind thirty years earlier. It's haphazard, a literal shot in the dark.

One of the soldiers points to a turret. We always get whoever does it, he says, and the next night there's always a new one.

In thirty days, he says, only one person inside the FOB has

been killed, an Afghan interpreter who was taking a shower when the shrapnel came through the stall.

Time and again, I'd hear throwaway stories of Afghan dead, often peppered into conversations as a means of conveying the seriousness of the situation without upending the narrative. It reminds me, in a way, of the ubiquitous scene in countless post-9/11 American war movies. In this scene, the protagonist, a morally upright sniper or checkpoint guard in a difficult situation, must choose whether to shoot dead a small Brown child or a woman in a niqab (*who's to say it's a woman at all, underneath that thing?*) who might be carrying some kind of suicide bomb. Surely any rational narrative assessment of the situation would conclude that the center of the story is not the sniper, but the person on the other side of the scope, whose life hangs in the balance. But the dead, unnamed, serve their purpose. It is the purpose of Westerners to contend with stakes, it is the purpose of everyone else to establish them.

At the FOBs I interview two Afghan soldiers. Kids, I can't help but think—eighteen, nineteen maybe. As was the case in many bases I visit, they're stationed at the outermost wire. In the larger bases, such as the NATO airfield in Kandahar, there's often an inner and outer wire. The inner wire protects the base proper, and then, after a middle space of chicanes and other barriers, the outer wire acts as the interface between the base and the wider world. As a result, it's almost always the outer wire that bears the brunt of the violence, of car bombs and ambushes. And it is almost always Afghans assigned to protect it.

One of the soldiers shows me his weapon: an AK, ancient-looking, almost a caricature of a gun.

They have body armor, they have good equipment, he says, why don't we? We protect this place.

I nod; I think about what Neil Sheehan once wrote in *A Bright Shining Lie,* about the difference between British and American approaches to empire—that the former felt compelled to civilize those they considered savage, a personal calling of sorts, a point of pride. The latter, on the other hand, had no use for any such notion. A strange thing, to be here, in this place, this moment, watching both costumes of empire thrown on at once.

Later that night, while walking from the mess hall to the sleeping quarters, we hear a whistling sound. I drop to the ground, as I'd been taught in hazardous environment training. I cover my ears. I breathe out the air in my lungs. I know I'm supposed to lie down such that my feet are closest to the point of impact, but I can't see anything.

The rocket lands up on the mountainside, harmless. We are, by virtue of luck, far enough away. And then the night sky lights up with the streaking red of tracer rounds. Someone sets off a flare and for a moment it is midday. And then silence. After a few seconds, one of the soldiers near me says something, a joke I don't catch, and everyone laughs to bleed out what's left of the adrenaline. Outside there's a body in the sand. Probably tomorrow there'll be another one.

The next morning, I leave. I escape consequence, as years later this entire enterprise would leave, would similarly escape.

•

It becomes impossible to accurately count the dead. The infrastructure that might have once done such a thing—the health ministry, the few functioning hospitals, the institutional fabric of society—is in ruins.

Language is never sufficient. There is not enough of it to make a true mirror of living. In this way, the soothing or afflictive effect of the stories we tell is not in whether we select the right words but in our proximity to what the right words might be. This is not some abstraction, but a very real expression of power—the privilege of describing a thing vaguely, incompletely, dishonestly, is inseparable from the privilege of looking away. Years ago, when I wrote a novel called *American War*, I found that one of the most popular uses of that phrase was as a Vietnamese moniker for what in the United States is called the Vietnam War. And what in the United States is now called the Civil War once had dozens and dozens of euphemistic names (of which one of the more memorable is the Late Unpleasantness).

In March 2013, while still working as a full-time reporter, I joined a team of Google employees on a trip to Iqaluit, the capital of Nunavut. The team was traveling there to map the far northern territory for Street View, the popular Google feature which allows users to virtually wander through much of the paved world.

It's a three-hour flight from southern Ontario to Iqaluit, a city of about 7,400 people. There's a hotel, a grocery store in which a few rolls of toilet paper went for something like $40, a shawarma place run by two Syrian guys—one who supported the Assad regime, one who didn't. It's small, isolated from and largely ignored by Canada's political power centers; it has one of the highest suicide rates in the world. For the Google team, this would be mostly a public relations exercise, similar to if not likely to be used as much as the Street View mapping of the trails on the Grand Canyon—*Look what we can do*. It was too expensive to ship the Street View car all the way up north, so instead the team brought a backpack with a long cylindrical attachment that rose about five feet into the air, a camera mounted on top. They'd map the place by foot.

On our second day in town, the company's engineers and PR people set up a meet-and-greet with the Indigenous elders of Iqaluit, mostly as a sign of respect but also because they had very concrete questions about the place—they'd never been there before, had no idea where to start.

What are the most important thoroughfares? one of them asked.

In winter or in summer? one elder replied.

It had not occurred to the Google mapmakers that what might be akin to a highway in December could turn to water in July. Their cognitive toolkit had no means of grappling with something like this. Until now, their lexicon had been sufficient to describe everything they deemed worth describing.

It may as well be the case that there exist two entirely different languages for the depiction of violence against victims of empire and victims *of* empire. Victims *of* empire, those who belong, those for whom we weep, are murdered, subjected to horror, their killers butchers and terrorists and savages. The rage every one of us should feel whenever an innocent human being is killed, the overwhelming sense that we have failed, collectively, that there is a rot in the way we have chosen to live, is present here, as it should be, as it always should be.

Victims of empire aren't murdered. Their killers aren't butchers, their killers aren't anything at all. Victims of empire don't die, they simply cease to exist. They burn away like fog.

To watch the descriptions of Palestinian suffering in much of mainstream Western media is to watch language employed for the exact opposite of language's purpose—to watch the unmaking of meaning. When *The Guardian* runs a headline that reads, "Palestinian Journalist Hit in Head by Bullet During Raid on Terror Suspect's Home," it is not simply a case of hiding behind passive language so as to say as little as possible, and in so doing risk as little criticism as possible. Anyone who works with or has even the slightest respect for language will rage at or poke fun at these tortured, spineless headlines, but they serve a very real purpose. It is a direct line of consequence from buildings that mysteriously collapse and lives that mysteriously end to the well-meaning liberal who, weaned on such framing, can shrug their shoulders and say, Yes, it's all so very sad, but you know, it's all so very *complicated.*

Some things are complicated. Some things have been complicated.

There is an art to this sort of thing. Of all the aftereffects of the War on Terror years, the most frequently underestimated is the heightened derangement of language for the purpose of sanitizing violence. It's a phenomenon that's by no means unique to that one moment in American history, but anyone who lived through the NATO invasion of Afghanistan and the decimation of Iraq will be familiar with the hallmark uses of this shadow vocabulary. No one, during those years, was ever tortured, only subjected to enhanced interrogation. When a soldier pulling at a joystick thousands of miles away mistook a wedding party for a terror cell and sent a missile-wielding drone to incinerate the lot, nobody was killed; there was only some collateral damage (a term first coined to describe the killing in Vietnam). No prisoners, who require a prison sentence, only detainees, who can be held forever without charge. And when those detainees, after years of confinement to cells not much bigger than broom closets, went on hunger strikes, they were engaged in "asymmetric warfare" against their captors.

It is easy enough to focus on the words, the phrases—their plain, malicious absurdity. But alone, words can only obscure so much. It is evident now, in this latest round of mass killing, that the machinery of state violence benefits just as greatly from the dehumanizing power of what is assumed as much as it does from what is said. The Bush- and Obama-era practice of labeling just about any man killed by the U.S. military as a terrorist until proven otherwise is one of the most pernicious policies to come of the post-9/11 years, and for good reason. It doubly defiles the dead, first killing then imposing upon them a designation they are no longer around to refute. It also renders them untouchable in polite society. Should a drone vaporize some nameless soul on the other side of the planet, who among us wants to make a fuss? What if it turns out they were a terrorist? What if the default accusation proves true, and we by implication are labeled terrorist sympathizers, ostracized, yelled at? It is generally the case that people are most zealously motivated by the worst plausible thing that could happen to them. For some, the worst plausible thing might be the ending of their bloodline in a missile strike. Their entire lives turned to rubble and all of it preemptively justified in the name of fighting terrorists who are terrorists by default on account of having been killed. For others, the worst plausible thing is being yelled at.

■

One day in 2008, while reporting from the military courtroom in Guantánamo Bay, I and a few other journalists were handed copies of a motion filed by one terror suspect's defense team. We had, by then, become used to the chessboard nature of these documents, full of black squares and rectangles that hid the things the military had deemed too dangerous for us to read, for the public to know. Officially, there existed a detailed formal guideline that was supposed to explain exactly why the military chose to withhold certain information, related almost always to matters of national security. But in reality, these explanations were often nonsense. There is a complex and fascinating psychology behind what gets blacked out—in the earliest editions of *Guantánamo Diary*, a book-length collection of the journals kept by Mohamedou Ould Slahi during his yearslong imprisonment, there is a scene in which he recounts being interrogated by several soldiers. The censors, before they would allow publication of the book, blacked out only the pronouns of the female soldier involved (eventually, in later editions, the sections were uncensored). In the motion we were handed that day in Gitmo, the thing blacked out was a copy of a *New York Times* article the defense lawyer had attached so the judge didn't have to go search it out himself. Someone had decided a story in the most well-known newspaper on the planet was too dangerous for us to read.

Allowed to wield silence so freely, any institution will become insatiable. It's not only that the absence of information allows those complicit in but unaffected by wrongdoing to look away. The silence itself becomes an empty canvas, onto which any fantasy can be painted. When every last Palestinian journalist has been killed, maybe there will never have been any Palestinian journalists at all. Maybe they will have all been terrorists or supporters of terrorists or whatever adjacency to terror is sufficient to scare off those who, in possession of something approximating a soul, might otherwise look upon such obvious assassination and say: This is wrong. Absent an act to describe and the language to describe it, we are capable of believing nothing, or multiple contradictory things, or anything at all.

There is, and has been for decades, a version of this phantom reality imposed on the Palestinian people, one in which they left their land willingly and were never expelled, never terrorized into movement. One in which, as Golda Meir stated and so many Israeli politicians have echoed since, there was no such thing as Palestinians. One in which Palestinian identity, if it did exist, was meaningless, and certainly conferred no rights. One in which these nonpeople were nonetheless treated well by the government and institutions that now rule over them, given good laborer jobs and sometimes even afforded free passage on the roads they're allowed to drive on and the buses they're allowed to board and behind the walls that are there purely to keep everyone safe. One in which every failed peace agreement is the fault of these intransigent, unreasonable people and not the state whose officials to this day gloat openly about never allowing a Palestinian state to exist. One in which every round of violence is the sole consequence of the last Palestinian act of violence. One in which tens of thousands of dead children have only their support of Hamas to blame—an organization that last won an election before those kids were born.

There's safety in this story, safety from one's own conscience. Because in this story the weight of indictment shifts onto the dispossessed, the disappeared, the dead, and one can continue as is, comfortable in the knowledge that history, narrative, language itself demands the killing continue. Or, better yet, has nothing to say at all.

If you visit Iqaluit on Street View today, you'll find a long unnamed road that juts out into the bay. In the pictures, the ground is ice. On the viewfinder, you'll be walking on water.

CHAPTER FIVE

RESISTANCE

To preserve the values of the civilized world, it is necessary to set fire to a library. To blow up a mosque. To incinerate olive trees. To dress up in the lingerie of women who fled and then take pictures. To level universities. To loot jewelry, art, banks, food. To arrest children for picking vegetables. To shoot children for throwing stones. To parade the captured in their underwear. To break a man's teeth and shove a toilet brush in his mouth. To let combat dogs loose on a man with Down syndrome and then leave him to die. Otherwise, the uncivilized world might win.

Guantánamo Bay, 2008:

There was supposed to be an art class, but the teacher never showed up. Either her security clearance never cleared or there was some illness. Or maybe she had second thoughts about traveling to an ad hoc prison camp in southeast Cuba to teach the basics of composition to a group of men the United States government had deemed the worst human beings on earth. Whatever the case, it fell on to one of the guards (who, if the charcoal rose on the easel was his, clearly had talent) to run the class. He would teach these men—maybe not the ones who'd earlier balled up their own shit and thrown it at him through the slot in their solitary cells to protest their detention, but others, the ones who'd been good—a little bit about art.

Our tour guide—our entire tour of the prison camp—fixates on these privileges afforded the "detainees," the myriad acts of altruism on the part of their captors. At Camp 4, the medium-security prison reserved for the most "compliant" captives, there's a small lending library. There are little rubber pens that bend so that they can't be used to stab; painted arrows on the ground pointing in the direction of Mecca; lines to hang laundry; a dirt soccer pitch. More than any of these things, though, the central privilege at Camp 4 is community—the prisoners are allowed to live alongside one another. In Camps 5 and 6—supermax facilities modeled after similar institutions in the mainland United States and constructed, according to a commemorative plaque out front, by Haliburton—"noncompliant" prisoners live in isolation cells for upward of twenty-three and a half hours a day. Inside the cells, near a small metal bed and toilet, there's a little coat hook on the wall. It's designed to flip downward if weighted too much, so that the prisoners are not able to hang themselves. It is in one of these camps that the art class was to be taught.

I travel to Guantánamo Bay on assignment eight times in 2008, mostly to cover the pretrial hearings of Omar Khadr. He's a Canadian who was captured after a firefight in Afghanistan and charged with killing a special forces medic. He was fifteen when he was captured and sent to Gitmo. He will spend the next decade of his life there, awaiting trial.

To report from Gitmo, journalists must first pass a security background check. Then, usually, they travel to Clinton, Maryland, and fly out of Joint Base Andrews. On my first trip, I arrive obscenely early, nervous to the point of shaking. But I encounter no trouble. At the gate I'm quickly let through and told to go to a nearby parking lot. I find a small bus waiting. Inside, there's a group of reporters who are all dressed far more formally than I have been told is normal for Gitmo. The bus driver asks me if I'm supposed to be on today's flight. I say yes. Inexplicably, he admonishes me for being late.

I get on, he starts driving. A few minutes later we pull onto the tarmac, right up to the stairs of Air Force One, and I realize I've gotten on the wrong bus. The way everyone's smiling faces change when they hear the sentence "Hi, my name's Omar and I'm not supposed to be flying with the president today" is a sight to behold.

The flight I eventually do get on, to Gitmo, takes longer than it would under normal circumstances. The plane is one of those sluggish Hercules transports, and rather than passing through Cuban airspace, it swoops around and comes in from the south. We arrive to a parcel of land that is neither fully Cuban nor American—a nowhere place in which one can build the flimsy scaffolding of a legal system outside the reach of the law.

A Guantánamo Bay military courtroom is a sanitized place. The reporters sit behind the glass, in a separate room, with an audio feed on delay that can be muted in case someone says something the judges deem classified. Myriad conventions and norms that would apply in most any other U.S. courtroom do not exist here. Names of key witnesses are withheld, evidence is withheld, hearsay is allowed. On one occasion, we watch a lawyer repeatedly admonished, then finally threatened with contempt, because he keeps repeating the name of a witness who he'd been ordered to refer to only by rank and initial. In most other courts, the name would be a matter of record, and the lawyer keeps reverting to what he knows of the law.

Over and over, the justification for all this—the secrecy and the censorship and the treatment of prisoners outside the realm of what the country's foundational legal principles would ever allow—is justified by the threat these prisoners are said to represent. In reality, the majority of them were never charged with anything, let alone convicted. Many of them the U.S. government freely admits were of no threat at all, wrongly imprisoned during the frenzy of those early War on Terror years.

(While working on Parliament Hill in Canada, I once chased a story about a group of Uyghurs, a Muslim minority long subjected to heinous abuse by the Chinese government. Fleeing this persecution, a few Uyghur men are picked up by Pakistani bounty hunters and sold to the Americans, who eventually ship them off to Gitmo. From early on, everyone involved comes to the conclusion that these men pose no threat at all, had simply been in the wrong place at the wrong time. Still, for years they languish on the island. They cannot be sent to China, where they will almost certainly be imprisoned and tortured, and they cannot be sent most anywhere else, since China threatens to make life politically miserable for any nation that takes them. For a while, there is some progress on transporting them to Canada, where there's at least a small Uyghur community. But then a Canadian man of Uyghur descent named Huseyin Celil is arrested while traveling in Uzbekistan and deported to China, where he is convicted of the kind of all-encompassing terrorism charges the Chinese government regularly throws at all manner of dissidents. The Canadian government eventually backs out of taking the Uyghurs from Gitmo, in part out of fear Celil might never leave his Chinese prison alive if they do. If he's still alive, Celil remains in prison to this day; his family hasn't heard from him in years.)

With relative (logistical, if not political) ease, pretty well every prisoner in Gitmo could all be transferred to facilities in the continental United States at any time, and the whole shameful legacy of the twenty-first century's most notorious prison camp be ended. And yet every time the idea is floated, a slew of lawmakers raise hell about the dangers of letting the most dangerous, evil people on the planet anywhere near the homeland. Almost a quarter century in, most of the prisoners are elderly now, frail and suffering from so many injuries and illnesses that one of the storerooms in Camp 5, when we visited, was packed full of artificial legs—but that doesn't matter. Whatever crimes they may have once been accused of, their mistreatment becomes, eventually, its own kind of self-perpetuating indictment. If they didn't hate the West before decades of their lives were taken from them, mustn't they hate it now? What is the statute of limitations on resentment, on rage, on revenge?

●

Among my hazier memories of early adolescence is a screening, at a friend's home, of an obviously pirated Betamax copy of *Red Dawn*. My friend's father—most everyone's father or mother or uncle, whoever—would, while on business trips overseas, visit the occasional video store or flea market and return with whatever films or books or albums they happened to find. It's a haphazard, incomplete thing to consume the culture of a faraway place in this manner, like trying to divine the contours of a mouth from the texture of spittle.

Red Dawn is a bad movie. Bad in a special, sincere kind of way. It's about a bunch of teenagers who fight back against a Soviet invasion of the United States. Released in the early eighties, it belongs to a large fraternity of films in which scrappy underdog Americans fight back against the seemingly insurmountable but of course ultimately very surmountable power of the Soviet empire. In a couple of decades, the Russians would pass the baton of villainy to people who look like me, though in our case there was no real empire to speak of, and so we were mostly small-batch insidious, our specialty less tank-and-jet and more suicide-bomb-level violence. It didn't much matter; *Red Dawn* with Arabs instead of Soviets for villains would have still been shit.

In 2012, almost thirty years after I first watched the original, someone decided to remake *Red Dawn*. This time, there was no Soviet empire to invade the mainland, and so instead the Chinese would have to do. Again, it didn't much matter—the point isn't geopolitical fidelity, the point is ninety minutes of rah-rahing American tenacity in the face of overwhelming odds. Never back down, never surrender, that sort of thing.

Problem is, China is a big market for movies. And so, at the last minute, for fear of missing out on millions in potential box office returns, the producers decided to change the villain. In the final cut of the *Red Dawn* remake, it's North Korea that invades the United States. It's always the sign of a well-crafted movie when you can change a central narrative beam in post and it doesn't make any difference at all. I'm reminded of a guy in one of my old writing groups who, fearing his story didn't have enough female representation, did a find-and-replace and changed every instance of "Sam" to "Samantha," then went through and changed the pronouns accordingly, leaving everything else the same.

Again, it didn't much matter. Except that it does, over time—this glaring disconnect between cultural self-image and pragmatic reality. In a 2016 essay, the writer and former soldier Roy Scranton describes watching *Star Wars* while stationed in Baghdad. He is forced in that moment to confront the reality that so much of the American self-image demands a narrative in which his country plays the role of the rebel, the resistance, when at the same time every shred of contemporary evidence around him leads to the conclusion that, by scope and scale and purpose of violence, this country is clearly the empire.

A central privilege of being of this place becomes, then, the ability to hold two contradictory thoughts simultaneously. The first being the belief that one's nation behaves in keeping with the scrappy righteousness of the underdog. The second being an unspoken understanding that, in reality, the most powerful nation in human history is no underdog, cannot possibly be one, but at least the immense violence implicit in the contradiction will always be inflicted on someone else.

I've seen this person many times—they occupy a hallowed place in American culture, catered to by so many of the nation's dominant cultural forces, from Monday Night Football to the Country Music Awards to the entirety of AM radio. It's the person who in self-image professes to be a rule-breaker, untamable, wild—and in the next breath sides unquestioningly with every facet of state power. I've seen the Punisher decal on the bumper, the stylized American flag denoting the thin blue line: *I'm an outlaw; also, anyone who disobeys the cops deserves to be killed.*

My first impulse is to mock the contradiction, but there's no contradiction, not really, because the bedrock of this particular identity isn't conformity or nonconformity—it's self-interest. Anyone who buys into both the narrative of American rebelliousness and the reality of American authority understands that both have been created to serve them. The man in the action movie looks one way, the man the cops just shot in a traffic stop another.

■

Toward the end of December 2023, the South African government brings charges of genocide against Israel at the International Court of Justice. The case rests on Israel's wholesale destruction of health facilities and the blocking of aid as evidence that what is being destroyed here isn't a single terror organization, but a whole people. Much of the initial South African brief relies on the words of Israeli officials themselves, including Prime Minister Benjamin Netanyahu's referencing of the complete destruction of Amalek in the Bible.

Among those who have been calling for an end to the relentless killing, the development inspires a set of conflicting emotions. First, there is the basic relief of watching some official entity—any entity—do something. Time and again, in conversation with friends, some of whom have lost family members in this killing spree, there is a sense that one must be going mad: to see so plainly the destruction, the murdered children filmed and presented for the world to look upon and then to hear the leaders of virtually every Western nation contend that this is not happening, that whatever is happening is good and righteous and should continue and that in fact the well-being of the Palestinian people demands this continue— it's enough to feel like you're losing your mind. As such, even were it a completely performative, hopeless act, the case brought before the International Court of Justice represents a brief respite from the bare-skinned duplicity, the Orwellian-ness of it all.

Second, there is the realization that of course it would be a country like South Africa that would take this step—a country deeply versed in the ugly mechanics of apartheid, for whose citizens checkpoints and forcefully sealed-off towns are not abstractions, but the very recent past that, from the safety of the present, everyone now claims they always opposed.

(I suspect every Arab knows it is a pipe dream to expect that Palestine's closest neighbors would be the ones to make this case before the International Court of Justice. For the gaggle of authoritarians who run most of the Arab world, there is nothing to be gained from meaningfully assisting a population so well versed in resisting oppression, lest that capacity for resistance prove contagious. There is, however, everything to be gained from empty sloganeering, and so when traveling through most every capital in the Arab world, one is greeted with massive Palestinian flags hanging from the buildings and across the billboards—and yet all this is coupled with the knowledge that, beyond placating the very real rage of the citizenry, there is very little impetus to do anything more substantive, to ruffle feathers, risk trade deals, provoke the ire of a superpower. If a ceasefire comes to pass, it might involve some behind-the-scenes maneuvering in Riyadh or Doha or Cairo, but one can't help but wonder how many Palestinians would still be alive today if the leaders of the Arab world thought of them as something more than slogan fodder.)

Beyond relief and recognition, there is a more complicated thing—an understanding that the machinery of the West has never had much of a capacity for self-diagnosis. Who does? Who that achieves power of this scale ever does?

Waiting on a Western judicial institution to cast judgment

on a killing spree financed and endorsed by the West means, inevitably, watching a disjointed ballet of impossible reconciling. The narrative—as enshrined in countless constitutions and declarations and charters which are so often held up as the differentiating marker of superiority of this world over the other—demands moral purity, opposition to injustice, adherence to the principle that all innocent lives are equal and deserving of dignity. The reality is that an ally of the West is killing civilians by the tens of thousands and it would be politically inconvenient to call this wrong now when for months, years, decades it has been deemed perfectly fine.

And so we must watch the impotent pantomime of a Canadian prime minister declaring that while his government absolutely supports the International Court of Justice, it doesn't support the premise of the South African case, whatever that tortured rhetorical construction is supposed to mean. We must watch the German government—whose police forces, in the name of fighting anti-Semitism, arrested Jewish protesters calling for a ceasefire—come to Israel's defense at the court.

In time there will be findings of genocide. There will be warrants issued, even. The structures of international law, undermined at every turn, will nonetheless attempt to operate as if law were an evenly allotted thing. As though criminality remains criminal even when the powerful support, bankroll, or commit the crime.

It's no use, in the end, to scream again and again at the cold, cocooned center of power: I need you, just this once, to be the thing you pretend to be.

There is an impulse in moments like this to appeal to self-interest. To say: These horrors you are allowing to happen, they will come to your doorstep one day; to repeat the famous phrase about who they came for first and who they'll come for next. But this appeal cannot, in matter of fact, work. If the people well served by a system that condones such butchery ever truly believed the same butchery could one day be inflicted on them, they'd tear the system down tomorrow. And anyway, by the time such a thing happens, the rest of us will already be dead.

No, there is no terrible thing coming for you in some distant future, but know that a terrible thing is happening to you *now*. You are being asked to kill off a part of you that would otherwise scream in opposition to injustice. You are being asked to dismantle the machinery of a functioning conscience. Who cares if diplomatic expediency prefers you shrug away the sight of dismembered children? Who cares if great distance from the bloodstained middle allows obliviousness. Forget pity, forget even the dead if you must, but at least fight against the theft of your soul.

■

In the summer of 2014, I began writing the first draft of my debut novel, *American War*. It's a piece of speculative fiction set in the 2070s and covers the aftermath of a second civil war. I never thought of it as a particularly American book, but rather an attempt to superimpose stories from the other side of the planet onto the heart of the empire. It didn't seem like a particularly clever narrative trick on my part.

Three weeks or so after I finished the first draft, Donald Trump announced his candidacy for president. The novel would end up being published in April 2017 and come to be almost universally read as an exclusively American story, a literal prediction of where this country might be headed. A bidding war breaks out for the film rights. Time and again, various production company executives tell me how perfectly the novel has managed to capture this moment in American life, and I can't help but think that the exact opposite is true. Something of American life has captured the novel. The word "dangerous" is used quite often, always as a compliment.

Then, in January 2024, I receive an email from the director who was set to work on the *American War* adaptation, letting me know he and the production company are stepping away from the project. "Prudence suggests this is not the time for making movies about freedom fighters or terrorists (no matter which side of that argument one is on)," he writes.

A few weeks earlier, a novelist I know tells me her appearance at a small book club has been canceled—the organizer tells her it's because they "stand with Israel." My friend is an American of half-Egyptian, half-Scottish descent. A Palestinian artist's retrospective at the University of Indiana is shuttered. People who call for a ceasefire are demoted, fired, called anti-Semites and terrorist-supporters.

It all feels so petty, the stakes so low. On the other side of the planet entire bloodlines are being wiped out and here in the sheltered world we are subject to relatively pathetic indignities—loss of income, disinvitations, cold shoulders from people who in a different time might have been quite proud of themselves for having a Brown friend. Every now and then we hear about those instances when the stakes turned out not to be so low, when this passive punishment transformed into something much more active, sometimes deadly. But for the most part it's just a constant trickle of reminders of one's place in the hierarchy—and it is precisely because of this that it becomes so tempting to just shut up, let what's going to happen happen to those people over there and then, when it's done, ease into whatever opinion the people whose approval matters deem acceptable.

I start to see this more often, as the body count climbs—this malleability of opinion. At a residency on the coast of Oregon, I read the prologue to this book; a couple of days later, one of the other writers decides to strike up a conversation.

"I'm not a Zionist," she says. "But you know, I'm not anti-Zionist either. It's all just so complicated."

I have no idea what to say. I feel like an audience at a dress rehearsal.

There's a convenience to having modular opinions; it's why so many liberal American politicians slip an occasional reference of concern about Palestinian civilians into their statements of unconditional support for Israel. Should the violence become politically burdensome, they can simply expand that part of the statement as necessary, like one of those dinner tables you lengthen to accommodate more guests than you expected. And it is important, too, that this amoral calculus rise and fall in proportion to the scale of the killing, so that one might always be able to say, "Well, we could never have known it would get this bad, but now, now everything has changed."

It's almost refreshing, then, when one is faced with the ugliest and yet most honest face of Western apathy, the face that knows full well the scale and severity of the horror but believes it to be absolutely justified, absolutely necessary. I know this face, too. It appears on talk shows and atop opinion pieces stating, euphemistically or not, that the same world in which you can buy avocados all year round and your iPhone keeps getting more powerful and you never have to live in fear of an occupying force obliterating your family with missiles is the world in which an insignificant group of people you'll never meet simply have to die. And whatever disgust this equation, laid bare, might inspire, many know it to be true. This is the world we've created, a world in which one privileged sliver consumes, insatiable, and the best everyone else can hope for is to not be consumed. It is not without reason that the most powerful nations on earth won't intervene to stop a genocide but will happily bomb one of the poorest countries on the planet to keep a shipping lane open.

(As a matter of tactics, it is instructive to know that Western power must cater to a sizable swath of people who can be made to care or not care about any issue, any measure of human suffering, so long as it affects the constant availability and prompt delivery of their consumables and conveniences. As a matter of moral health, the same knowledge is horrifying.)

How long can the fabric of a pleasing story hold? Presented the facts of the situation without label, without real-world anchor, like actors asked to read the screenplay and pick a role, how many Americans would instinctively choose that of the Palestinian calling for an end to occupation? The South African calling for an end to apartheid? The Haitian calling for self-rule? How many would want to believe, as so much of the culture here has always strained to believe, that they side with the underdog, the downtrodden who refuses to give up, the rebel in the face of empire? And then, should the scenes be transposed back to the unforgiving reality of the world as it is, how many, knowing the limitations of the stories we tell ourselves, would just as instinctively retreat into the comforting fold of empire?

CHAPTER SIX

CRAFT

On a British television network, a newscaster describes the scene at an Israeli checkpoint: "Accidentally, a stray bullet found its way into the van ahead, and that killed a three- or four-year-old young lady."

It was tragic, he says.

Cairo, 2010:

What I tell my editor, seven time zones away in Toronto, is that I'm going to run to an interview. What I do is go visit my father's grave.

They die young, the men I come from: my father at fifty-six, his father around the same age. One night, in August 2010, I get a call from my mother in Italy, where she'd been vacationing with my father. He'd suffered a heart attack; they were in a hospital in Naples, it was touch-and-go. A short while later, a second call.

Grief becomes an aperture for the hours, time slides through and stills. I travel to Italy. I help my mother prepare my father's body for transport and burial. In Islamic tradition, there is a ritual washing of the dead; a group of local Muslims in Naples offer to do it. Afterward, we fly, the three of us, back to Egypt, our first flight together since we came to Canada, all those years ago. I pray over my father's body aside strangers in the Rabaa al-Adawiya Mosque as he undertakes the last of his leavings and arrives finally back home.

He had always wanted to be buried in Egypt, in the El Akkad mausoleum where my step-aunts and grandfather are buried. And so we take him there. I crawl on my hands and knees into the catacomb. I help ease the shrouded body to the ground, beside the bones of these people who loved him from the day he was born. Outside, dozens of our relatives stand waiting, people I love similarly and who love me and with whom, in another life where we never left, I would have shared the normal bonds of family. Instead, they appear to me now as foreigners, because we did leave. And so it has only ever been, for me, the three of us. Now we are two. The absence is seismic, something of the ground beneath me coming apart.

We return to Canada. I fly west and clean out my father's apartment. There are only a few clothes to collect, a block of cheese and some bread to throw out, a single volume from Al-Isfahani's *Book of Songs*, my father's favorite work of literature. Smears of living.

Two years later, I return to Egypt for the first time since my father's burial. This time, I'm dispatched there by my newspaper. I intend to cross into Gaza to cover yet another round of shelling by the Israeli military, but the day after I land in Cairo, then president Mohamed Morsi helps broker a ceasefire. As far as the foreign desk is concerned, the story is dead. But then, a few days later, Morsi issues a set of decrees giving himself largely unchecked powers until the country's new constitution is finalized. The move spurs widespread protest, on which the military eventually piggybacks. It becomes, overnight, one of the biggest stories in the world, and by the strange and often grotesque journalists' definition of luck, I am there to cover it.

One night, after filing my story, I go for a ride around town with an old high school friend. We drive aimlessly, past the heavily guarded residence of the president, past the abandoned half-constructed buildings, past cafés ringed with colored incandescents, these forgotten artifacts of my earliest memories. I ask my friend how the years following the Arab Spring have been for him, and he shakes his head.

Everything's falling apart, he says.

I had heard the same sentiment before, from many members of my family—Egypt's precarious upper middle class, for whom democracy was a nice abstraction, but the janitor's son getting all worked up and forgetting his place was very, very real. With a strong, decisive man at the helm, you have stability, I was told time and again—not this chaos where all norms and values go out the window, and who knows what your kids end up thinking or saying or doing. Years later, I'd hear all this again on a different assignment, interviewing Trump voters.

Two years after millions of people risked their lives to

overthrow a despot, something had soured. Performative praise of the revolution by politicians and business leaders masked an attempt (ultimately successful) to undo everything the revolutionaries fought for; Western leaders who'd been so vocal in support of freedom and democracy returned to the serious business of backing whichever entity best suited their interests. It was not particularly new: we'd all watched George W. Bush declare that Islam isn't the enemy as he launched an illegal war that left hundreds of thousands of predominantly Muslim civilians dead. Twenty years later, we'd all watch a smirking White House press secretary claim that no one has done more for the Palestinians, as the same White House helped facilitate their eradication.

During the time I reported from Egypt, I had started work on *American War*. In one scene in the book, the United States, amid complete institutional collapse, is visited by the president of a new pan-Arab empire. The president delivers a speech venerating the two nations' shared desire for basic democratic rights. Years later, after I sold the manuscript, one of my editors returned the section to me and suggested it would hit harder if the speech itself were not so transparently insincere, if it seemed the head of this empire had at least some belief in the platitudes he was espousing. I had copied the text, almost word for word, from Barack Obama's 2009 speech in Cairo, the one titled "A New Beginning."

It's all fiction, I understand—the novel, the speech within it, maybe the other speech too. But so long as there exists a Western self-conception that demands the appearance of purity at all times, it should be known that what shocks the most isn't the cruelty or indifference. Many people's governments are cruel, many people's governments are indifferent. It's this relentless parachuting of virtue. It's these speeches and statements of eloquently stated concern for human rights and freedom and the demand that those who abuse human rights or withhold freedom be held to account. And it's the way every ideal turns vaporous the moment it threatens to move beyond the confines of the speeches and statements, the moment it threatens even the most frivolous parcel of self-interest.

What good are words, severed from anything real?

●

In early November 2023, at a literary prize ceremony in Toronto, a group of young people upend the proceedings. One storms the stage, calling for a ceasefire. As far as disruptive protests go, it's about as straightforward and unobtrusive as one can get, short of not protesting at all.

The Giller Prize is presented yearly to a Canadian novelist, along with a check for $100,000. It has launched, revived, or saved the careers of many writers in its thirty-year history, mine included. Most years, the prize is awarded at the end of a lavish ceremony in a downtown Toronto hotel. As a former winner, I'm invited to attend the ceremony where the protest ends up taking place. At the last minute, I decide to stay home. Writers do lonely work. Most of us don't get to see each other all that often, and when we do, it sure as hell isn't at the Four

Seasons. But I can't bring myself to do it, to put on the tuxedo and pick at the canapés and smile and be nice, at all costs *be nice*. I can't bring myself to celebrate. I know there's likely going to be a particular politician there who, days earlier, glibly voted against even a symbolic UN resolution calling for a ceasefire and then went on social media to post a paean to the beauty of Shakespearean sonnets. I'm afraid if I run into him I might not be able to keep from sounding like the angry Arab man every Arab man is secretly believed to be. Nothing good can come of it, I don't think. Or maybe something good can come of confronting this man and people like him, people who know empathy can always be faked in hindsight so long as the bad thing is happening to someone else—and maybe I'm too scared to find out. Those people who storm the stage are not.

I hear about the protest the next day. It's the usual stuff: how rude these young people are, to disrupt an evening meant to celebrate writers and writing; how this sort of inconveniencing of people's good time is only likely to turn public opinion against the demonstrators' cause (if nothing else at all, the protest sheds light on something I and most everyone in the ballroom that night probably didn't know: that the Giller Prize's corporate sponsor, one of Canada's biggest banks, held a $500 million stake in an Israeli weapons maker).

A day or two later, a writer friend of mine emails asking if I'd sign an open letter. The letter calls for charges to be dropped against the protesters, for a ceasefire in Gaza, and for the release of the hostages held by Hamas and in "administrative detention" by Israel. I sign it, I don't think twice. It seems quite literally the least I can do. What happened at the Four Seasons feels like exactly what young people—what *people*—should do when they believe an injustice is taking place.

But the literary community, especially in Canada, isn't all that large. The letter sets off a small firestorm of newspaper articles and rival open letters. I suppose it makes sense: people were made momentarily uncomfortable at a black-tie gala— someone has to pay.

Watching footage of the demonstration later, what fascinates me isn't the smattering of boos from the audience as the protesters take to the stage, it isn't even the protest itself—it's all the people in that room, so many of them either involved in or so vocally supportive of literature, who keep their heads down, say nothing, wait for it all to just be done. A room full of storytellers, and so many of them suddenly finding common cause in silence.

I want so desperately to believe that, were I in the ballroom that night, I would have done something different. Maybe I wouldn't have, maybe I would have been silent too. I heard once about a psychology experiment in which the subject is sent into a room with nine other people and told that in a minute everyone will be asked a simple question: How many people are in this room? The subject doesn't know that the other nine people have been instructed to answer eleven. The subject is always asked last and the subject, overwhelmingly, says eleven.

What is the work writers do? Not the writing, not the thing that lives on—the work, the inward conversation that must be had again and again and again before even a modicum of meaning arrives on the page. I used to have, in my back pocket, an answer, many answers. Some dwelled on the obligation to make fire from the sparks human friction expels, or some other nonsense meant to give me some kind of north star when completely lost in the valleys of some disastrous manuscript. Or at least something that sounds good in a craft talk. In truth, I have no idea what the work really is, and yet I find myself returning to the question time and again, as I watch some of the quietest, most demure, most inward-looking writers I know—writers I always thought of as obsessed exclusively with the *work*—act as the most vocal opponents of genocide. Meanwhile, writers who until recently were downright apocalyptic about cancel culture and the necessity of "writing outside yourself" and the epidemic of silencing that plagues our craft suddenly turn awful quiet.

I don't know what this work is anymore. I read piece after lengthy, erudite piece about the need for a nuanced, both-sides discussion of a genocide, about how words are so easily weaponized, and we must be very careful because weapons can hurt—as all the while very real weapons raze entire Palestinian neighborhoods and their occupants. A magazine decides to pull a milquetoast essay that reads like an Israeli settler-colonial homage to *The Blind Side,* and writers line up to condemn the existential threat this kind of censorship represents to the future of literature itself. Fine: What does the killing of hundreds of Palestinian novelists, poets, and journalists mean for the future of literature? I read an op-ed in which a writer argues that the model for Palestinian-Israeli coexistence is something like Canada's present-day relationship with the Indigenous population, and I marvel at the casual, obvious, but unstated corollary: that there is an Indigenous population being colonized, but that we should let this unpleasantness run its course so we can arrive at true justice in the form of land acknowledgments at every Tel Aviv poetry reading. And yet there's at least a banal honesty about it. Some of the least established writers I know, the ones who have to work all manner of side jobs just to make ends meet, are actively putting their literary careers at risk by calling for an end to the wholesale murder of a people. Meanwhile, so many of the most established writers are either totally silent or engaged in the tritest finger-wagging about just how terrible it would be for the art if we get too shrill about this sort of thing. Yes, the killing happens now, but there'll be plenty of time later to write very moving stories about the shape and shade of the bones.

Maybe there never was work, only a passing through time and consequence. Maybe we don't read writers so much as become deeply acquainted with the sites of their passing, or their refusal to pass. What they thought beautiful or grotesque enough to document. Where they chose to expend their finite capacity for concern.

■

In mid-October 2023, the Frankfurt Book Fair decides to cancel a ceremony in which the Palestinian writer Adania Shibli was to be presented with an award for her novel *Minor*

Detail. The book is based on the true story of a Bedouin Palestinian girl raped and murdered by Israeli soldiers. Later, the organizers will claim the decision to cancel the award was made jointly with the author (it wasn't) and that the awards ceremony was not canceled, only indefinitely postponed. Looking back, the cancellation marks one of the earliest instances of what would become a cascade of institutional gutlessness in the arts world. Over the next few months, book clubs would preemptively prohibit questions about Palestine in their events. An academic article by Rabea Eghbariah on the Nakba—the calamitous, violent expulsion of Palestinians from their own land in 1948—set to be published in the *Harvard Law Review* is pulled at the last minute. When the *Columbia Law Review* agrees to publish the article, and refuses pressure from its own board of directors to delete it, the board takes the journal's entire website down. The Pulitzer Prize, which in previous years issued special citations to the journalists of Ukraine and Afghanistan, will instead commend the work of "Journalists and Media Workers Covering the War in Gaza"— avoiding the word "Palestinian" altogether. A memo from the standards editor at *The New York Times,* leaked to *The Intercept,* cautions against using the word "Palestine."

I remember once sitting on a panel at a literary festival that began with an organizer doing a bit of housekeeping. First and foremost, he told the audience, it is important that we acknowledge we are on unceded Indigenous land . . . and thank the hedge fund that has generously sponsored this event. It might be one of the most unintentionally honest land acknowledgments I've ever heard.

Writing is a precarious profession. We are broke, for the most part. We work jobs we often don't enjoy to keep the lights on: Faulkner at the post office, Vonnegut and his disastrous car dealership, every writer you know and their faculty gig. The average author doesn't make enough from their royalties to clear the poverty line. Most books don't even make back their advance, meaning they earn no royalties for the author at all. When Anna Burns won the Booker Prize, she thanked her food bank. Our work is stolen to train the software of multibillion-dollar artificial intelligence companies run by people who believe art is a problem to be solved.

And so we come to rely on the graces of grants and fellowships and residencies and awards. We play nice because, well, why not? It's exhausting, being difficult all the time. So what if that debut novel prize is paid for by a company actively destroying independent bookstores? So what if the fellowship is named after a marauding captain of industry? When you really think about it, what *isn't* named after one of those guys? If by not playing nice, one misses out on the resources needed to do the writing in the first place, is the trade-off really worth it? The Renaissance artists had their many-castled benefactors, why can't we have ours?

Because sometimes the powerful commit or condone or bankroll acts of unspeakable evil, and any institution that prioritizes cashing the checks over calling out the evil is no longer an arts organization. It's a reputation-laundering firm with a well-read board.

But amid the cowardice, there are moments of solidarity. When a rich donor tries to scare the National Book Foundation by pulling financial support after hearing that some of the nominees plan to use the National Book Award stage to call for a ceasefire, the foundation doesn't flinch. When PEN America does almost nothing to address in any meaningful way the mass killing of Palestinian writers, almost all the authors nominated for the organization's literary awards decline them—walking away from substantial prize money. The organization eventually has to cancel the awards ceremony altogether. At a workshop where I occasionally teach in Portland, the director of the program begins the week with a land acknowledgment that also mentions Gaza even as he admits that all of this feels particularly ineffectual right now. A friend of mine who runs an online writing college gives teachers the option to donate residuals from their craft videos to a charity providing aid to Palestinians. It all feels so small and yet I hold on to it dearly, all of it, every effort, no matter how symbolic—not only for reasons of basic humanity but for more selfish reasons, too. As though with these smallest gestures I can, if not answer, at least keep at bay the question that returns alongside every new wave of unchecked atrocity: What is this work we do? What are we good for?

"I want to be like those poets who care about the moon,"

the Palestinian American poet Noor Hindi writes. The poem is titled "Fuck Your Lecture on Craft, My People Are Dying."

In almost every craft talk I've ever given, I find myself returning to Hemingway's Iceberg principle—the notion that the vast majority of what is known about a story should exist beneath the surface of that story, unseen. It's one of the most well-worn pieces of writing advice, a close cousin of the directive "Show, don't tell." Most every MFA student has heard some variation, and I have no strong feelings about whether they follow it or not. My interest is in feasibility. It's one thing to adhere to this business of not saying when one maintains some sense of belonging within the canon, within things previously said. When one can name their story *The Sun Also Rises,* knowing that the Book of Ecclesiastes is not an obscure text. It's another thing entirely to pull from without, from some other lineage, and expect the unsaid to resonate, to be similarly understood. Maybe this is all the kind of pedantic nerdery writers obsess about all the time, but I can't help but think of it now in the context of the killing fields, whose dead also belong to some other lineage. I think of the hundreds upon hundreds of pictures and videos of the mutilated, the starved, the dismembered, and I am reminded that all of this is functionally invisible to so many in the part of the world where I now live. That if it were presented to them, some would undoubtedly respond the way Barbara Bush once did when asked about the Iraqi dead: "Why should we hear about body bags and deaths? It's not relevant. So why should I waste my beautiful mind on something like that?" But others, I think, would recoil in a different way. Stubborn as anything, I hang on to the hope that, presented with proof of injustice, the majority human reflex is to act against it.

And then I think of a line that has always stayed with me, from Marwa Helal's "poem for brad who wants me to write about the pyramids":

> *this is where the*
> *poets will interject*
> *they will say: show, dont tell*
> *but that*
> *assumes most people*
> *can see.*

It would be nice to go back to caring about the moon. So many of my favorite authors care about the moon. So much of my favorite literature orients in the direction of beauty. But surely any true appreciation of beauty would admit, exclaim even, that no description of the moon, no matter how stunning, how true, reflects as much beauty back into the world as a missile obliterating a family in their home takes out of it.

At the very least, one should not be able to have it both ways. One should not, with a modicum of self-respect, quote Morrison and Baldwin at every turn but then, faced with the sort of injustice with which so much of their work contends, suddenly retreat into descriptions of whatever it is the finches are doing.

What is this work we do? What are we good for?

The literary critic Northrop Frye once said all art is metaphor, and a metaphor is the grammatical definition of insanity. What art does is meet us at the site of our insanity, our derangement, the plainly irrational mechanics of what it means to be human. There comes from this, then, at least a working definition of a soul: one's capacity to sit with the mysteries of a thing that cannot in any rational way be understood— only felt, only moved through. And sometimes that thing is so grotesque—what we do to one another so grotesque—that sitting with it feels an affront to the notion of art as a conduit of beauty.

Still, sit. Sit.

CHAPTER SEVEN

LESSER EVILS

The cartoon character on her shirt is still visible. Her face is not. She'd hurt no one.

Simi Valley, 2015:

At the Ronald Reagan Presidential Library, perched in the mountains about thirty miles north of Malibu, there's a glass-walled hangar with a replica of Air Force One. The visitors center, a wide terra-cotta-tiled building, is postcard middle California. Serene against a manicured lawn, it's prettiest at sunset, when the dips of land in the distance turn honey and gold. There's a replica section of the Berlin Wall, and a podium people can stand at and pretend to give speeches.

In September 2015 I come here to watch the Republican Party try to pick a presidential nominee. It's early days, the field still full of plainly hopeless candidates—so much so that there's a "kiddie debate" undercard before the main event. It's an embarrassing affair in which all the people who have so far polled in the single digits talk over one another the same way the higher-polling candidates will in a few hours, trying to leave a smear of their names and faces in the memory of the audience. These are people who know they will never win. Likely they want cabinet positions, or simply to improve their prospects for future runs. Some are rich enough to self-fund vanity campaigns. In the media room, some of the reporters bristle at having to pay any attention to these people. We wait on the spectacle of consequence.

The main event sees a CNN moderator lob questions at nine Republican hopefuls, all of whom take turns doing the sort of thing Republicans have been doing for most of the twenty-first century, painting the United States as simultaneously the greatest country on earth and a nightmare place. An enormously powerful, God-chosen nation in which families are too scared to leave their houses at night. There is a desperate tinge to this pantomime, because eight of these nine people are starting to understand that they cannot win; that no matter how much red meat they throw out, they are still unable to give the party's base what it craves. The only man who doesn't have this problem is Donald Trump. He is armored in a baseness the other candidates simply don't know how to wear. He understands what his opponents don't—that the people who will decide this election have gone well past red meat. They want the body served up alive.

After the debate, the reporters scrum with party insiders. I listen to Reince Priebus, the chair of the GOP, go on at length about Newt Gingrich. The relevance of Gingrich to an election in the year 2015 seems unclear until I realize the point Priebus is trying to make. Decades earlier, Gingrich too was leading in the early primary polls, before his campaign collapsed.

Priebus, like most Republican Party insiders, hates Donald Trump. It is an ongoing mockery of the entire Republican establishment that this man is so thoroughly humiliating what Priebus and his ilk have tried to paint as the deepest, most qualified lineup of candidates in American history. And so Priebus wants us all to know, to believe, that this early momentum won't last. Order will be restored. The glaring chasm between the dignified thing Republicanism pretends to be and the exclusively hate-catering thing it really is will soon stop being so glaring.

Within a few months, most every one of these party insiders will roll over, pledge fealty to a man they privately despise. There's no avenue but him to power, and no principle worth holding on to in power's stead.

There was a time, mostly forgotten now, when almost every centrist institution in this country bent over backward to describe Donald Trump's appeal as a function of some kind of "economic anxiety." The alternative—that millions of Americans want desperately for people who don't look and live and believe the way they do to suffer without end—was too unpleasant to consider, too much an indictment of something bigger than one man's campaign. Even years later, as the same man, now convicted or indicted for a litany of crimes, still easily controls the base of the Republican Party, there is great care on the part of many mainstream liberals to focus on the destructive potential of Trump as a singular entity, a freak storm somehow returned to shore, rather than a symptom of an entirely different climate.

This chasm between the thing one pretends to be and the thing one really is—it's not an exclusively Republican phenomenon.

●

I remember when the fires came to Oregon. It was September 2020, just two days after the birth of our son. We sat in the living room with our bags packed, multiple air purifiers running. Through the windows, we couldn't see thirty feet to the edge of the backyard. The sky had turned a deep, unnatural copper. A layer of ash covered everything.

In Clackamas County, one of the hardest hit, entire towns were wiped off the face of the earth. It was the most destructive blaze the Pacific Northwest had ever seen. Even years later, I can drive a half hour south of my house, across the river that spared us, and pass through places of which all that remain are chimneys and piping, the trees thin and black as quills all along the hillside.

For about two years, my internal marker for where the ruined part of the county began was the scorched corpse of a pickup truck by the side of Highway 22, nothing left of it but the chassis, and from the remains of the bed, a huge Trump flag flying.

The political topography of Oregon isn't all that different from a lot of the United States—venture outside the big cities and things take a hard right turn. On election day in 2016 we woke to find the convenience store down the road had littered its back lawn with hundreds of Trump signs, so weirdly gridlike in their arrangement that the grounds took on the feel of a cemetery. Once, while on the search for a hiking trail that follows an abandoned railway track near Nehalem River, my friend and I stumbled onto a makeshift firing range in the forest. There were little printed headshots of Hillary Clinton taped to the targets. By landmass, Oregon, like many states, is deep red; some of the biggest, most sparsely populated counties go Republican in a landslide.

Among the more troubling trends of twenty-first-century American politics is the normalization of every election as the existential one, the one upon whose results rests the very survival of American democracy. In one way or another, there is some truth to this claim. Almost without fail, whatever deranged position sat on the periphery of the Republican Party a decade ago now resides in the center. Does anyone truly believe the same party, in another decade's time, will be more moderate and reasonable? When will any Democratic candidate not be able to say: *Elect me or they will dismantle everything, will wreak unimaginable havoc, unbelievable cruelty.*

However true it may be, there's also an aggrandizing quality to this kind of framing. It appeals to the liberal version of the *Red Dawn* reflex. In a perfect world, politics is boring, informed by debate but assured of a mutual understanding that the civic good matters. It's tree-cutting permits and public transport levies and people who go to school for years and years to learn how to best pass a thoroughfare through a residential area. Republicanism, in its current form, proposes the exact opposite—treason trials for political opponents, the stripping away of any societal covenant, a war on expertise. In the right-wing vision of America, every societal interaction is an organ harvest, something vital snatched from the civic body, sold for one kind of profit or another. It's a vision that produces an almost unmatched clarity in the base, an unmatched loyalty: *Which side of this operation do you want to be on?*

In mid-January 2024, with Gaza's health system essentially collapsed and no one left to count the dead, *The New York Times* publishes an article detailing a drop in the number of Palestinian casualties—marking a change in Israel's approach, it is said. This will happen again and again in the coming months: very serious reporting about perceived slowdowns in the rate of killing, the "war" entering a different "phase."

Every such story seems to prompt another round of argument about the folly of abandoning the Democratic Party now, when so much is at stake. A writer friend of mine describes it as cutting off your nose to spite your face. It's a hackneyed phrase for a writer to rely on, but I can't stop thinking about it, the privilege implicit in its assumptions: ownership of body, agency over mutilation.

It is a source of great confusion first, then growing rage, among establishment Democrats that there might exist a sizable group of people in this country who quite simply cannot condone a real, ongoing genocide, no matter how much worse an alternative ruling party may be or do. This stance boggles a particular kind of liberal mind because such a conception of political affairs, applied with any regularity, forces the establishment to stand for something. It suddenly becomes insufficient to say: Elect us or else they will abolish abortion rights; elect us or they will put more migrants in concentration camps; elect us or they will make your lives so much worse. What is the use, once elected, of doing anything of substance when what was necessary, the negation of some other hypothetical outcome, has by definition already been achieved?

We know it could be worse. We have been made to know. The parents whose children were stolen from them at the border under the direction of the Trump administration were not hypothetical (though such policies didn't begin with Trump, and didn't end after). The Muslims who had to watch loved ones die from afar because they could not leave or enter the country on account of a plainly racist law were not hypothetical. But neither were those kids a drone mistook for terrorists. Neither were those people killed by bad cops and left to drown by border agents and told—but, thank God, by a more liberal administration this time—those new oil-drilling leases are the best thing for their children's future. And neither are the tens of thousands of people being shot and bombed and left to die cold and hungry when a single directive from the White House could end it.

It is an admirable thing, in a politics possessed of a moral floor, to believe one can change the system from the inside, that with enough respectful prodding the establishment can be made to bend, like that famous arc, toward justice. But when, after decades of such thinking, decades of respectful prodding, the condition one arrives at is reticent acceptance of genocide, is it not at least worth considering that you are not changing the system nearly as much as the system is changing you?

A few months into the genocide, protesters are regularly interrupting Democratic Party events. Dozens of major universities across the country come to a standstill as students build encampments to protest the killing. It harkens most clearly to the anti-apartheid movement of the eighties and the antiwar and civil rights protests of the sixties—all of them, too, led overwhelmingly by young people and derided as naive and inconsequential until they weren't, until they became central facets of the story the United States tells itself about how, inevitably, justice prevails.

Once again, the party's supporters react to these demonstrations by chanting "Four more years, four more years," which by now can no longer be described as simply ghoulish. There is instead a kind of mechanical fear laced in it, a sense among these people, as there has been a sense among all people at all times on whom the judgment of future historians has started to dawn, that they have stepped too far into complicity with something evil.

Look up photographs of what we now consider this country's—any country's—most morally diseased moments. The dogs being let loose on men and women asking for basic dignity, the marching of undesirables through the streets, the wrath, the bloodlust. Ignore, for a moment, the people engaged most directly in the violence. Look instead at the faces of those who watch from the sidelines. Often, what you'll find is not an expression of proud support or the shock and horror all these people will claim to have felt much later, after the verdict is in. Rather, you'll see a childish little smirk. It's the smirk of someone who has come to realize the ugliness of the enterprise they have passively aligned with but cannot muster the courage to abandon now. The soul, what's left of it, buckles under the weight of contradiction, and all one can do is hide behind that pained little smirk, the half-stance of the spineless, the chanting, with not quite enough conviction, of four more years, four more years, as the bodies pile up outside one's door.

It's difficult to live in this country in this moment and not come to the conclusion that the principal concern of the modern American liberal is, at all times, not what one does or believes or supports or opposes, *but what one is seen to be*. From this outcome, everything is reverse-engineered. Being seen as someone who believes in justice—not the messy, fraught work of achieving it—is the starting point of any conversation on justice. Saying the right slogans supersedes whatever it is those slogans are supposed to oblige. It makes sense—when there are no real personal stakes, when the missiles are landing on someone far away, being seen as good is good enough.

But there were always going to be consequences. The fascists whose ranks exert such outsize influence on Republican politics have come to understand that the veneer of liberalism is a deeply vulnerable thing. Its perfunctory concern with rhetorical evenhandedness gives even the most obviously bad-faith allegation influence. The result is an endless stream of distractions, fantastical claims, and charges on which, in the name of fairness, countless ink is spilled, debates had. Again, what matters is not the damage done when such nonsense is given oxygen, but the idea of being a person who gives all ideas a fair shake.

Beyond the stream of distractions, there is a much more existential vulnerability. Whatever derangement currently occupies conservative American politics is, at least, something of very real consequence: the minority groups they want to legislate out of every facet of society, the books they want to ban, the mechanisms of democracy they want to subvert— none of it is hypothetical. But if inoffensive centrism is seen to be concerned with these things only in as far as it reflects on the centrist's self-image, if the Hillary Clintons of the world can muster great outrage at the fortunes of the *Barbie* movie at the Oscars but nothing at population-wide military murder sprees, then every Republican will always be able to say, truthfully: *At least there's no contradiction between what I am, what I claim concerns me, and what I plan to do.*

This is the crux of it, the unavoidable reckoning. Every morning countless well-paid, well-educated foot soldiers in the employ of the Democratic Party wake up and decide on the day's talking points. Every morning a small army of spokespeople step to the lecterns and deliver statements about how much the president cares for innocent lives, or the immense effort the United States makes to minimize unnecessary suffering, or whatever it is that needs to be said that day so as to launder the evil done between the last press conference and this one. A growing number of people ask a different question; the world asks a different question. The world, full of people who factor not one iota in the calculus of those morning meetings, looks upon this and asks, simply: Beyond self-interest, what do you believe in? And every morning the answer, dressed up in anesthetic euphemism and dependent on our collective capacity for resignation to the lesser of two evils, is: Nothing.

On January 26, 2024, the International Court of Justice rules that Israel must stand trial for genocide. Not long after, the United States, Canada, the United Kingdom, and six other nations decide to cut off all funding to the United Nations Relief and Works Agency, one of the few organizations providing any aid to Palestinians. The decision is supposedly based on allegations that about a dozen of the UNRWA's 30,000 or so workers were involved in the October 7 Hamas attacks. The allegation is enough. Hundreds of millions of dollars are withheld. More people will starve to death because of this decision, taken in the halls of power far away from where the starvation will happen, taken by people who will never be held responsible for any of it, who will live out the rest of their lives in total comfort. And should some activist interrupt their night out at a restaurant to show them pictures of the children they've helped kill, they will be deeply offended. Civilized people shouldn't behave so rudely.

—

I went to a Trump rally once, in Eugene. People sold pins and shirts and other paraphernalia in the parking lot, most of it stamped with stuff like, LOCK THE BITCH UP. A mostly naked young woman protested at the intersection closest to the venue; a few college kids living nearby put up signs on their lawns saying, FUCK TRUMP. Not a single unexpected thing happened.

Except later, midway through Trump's speech. He showed up late, meandered as usual, seemed fully lost at times, or not lost but bored, bored with these people who had nothing to give him but the very temporary sugar rush of adoration. He tried various bits on for size, about murderous immigrants and how America isn't winning anymore. Eventually, even the most enthusiastic in the crowd sensed their leader's heart wasn't really in it, that he bristled at having to play this no-name open mic when what he really wanted was Madison Square Garden. And then, quietly, a few walked out. The die-hards stayed but a smattering of people who'd until then stood there, smirks on their faces, began to leave.

A few days after the ICJ decision, Nancy Pelosi floats the theory that some of the people who are calling for a ceasefire have Russian ties. Later she'll add China to the mix—the real source of this phantom treason of not much concern, in the grand scheme of things. The carefree quality of the accusation, the ease with which it can be lobbed, is as powerful as the accusation itself. Anyone who came to the West from the places where such charges are commonplace recognizes it immediately. In the country of my birth, where, as of this writing, inflation rages somewhere around 130 percent and a substantial portion of the population doesn't have enough to eat, everything is the fault of an insidious plot hatched by Israelis and Americans, by the West, by some outsider jealous of Egypt's potential or intent on its destruction. It's a prized tool in almost every failed regime's workshop. It's a source of great disillusionment, to see it so casually repurposed by a democratically elected Western politician.

Does Nancy Pelosi truly believe that the countless state and county offices of her own party that have called for a ceasefire are aligned with the Russians? Unions representing millions of American workers? The city council of Chicago? All of them agents of hostile foreign powers who have chosen this particular issue to unleash their Manchurian candidates? She doesn't. Just as when she calls for the FBI to investigate activists protesting for a ceasefire, the message's primary audience isn't the FBI or the activists, it's the base. It is to say, to the centrist who simply cannot understand why a good upstanding student at Columbia would risk their job prospects to protest some distant unpleasantness: These people making trouble are not like you. If they get their way, things will change and it will not be to your benefit.

One struggles to determine the more frightening reality: that this message is a lie, or that it's true.

I watch an interview with Representative Alexandria Ocasio-Cortez, Democrat of New York. "I think, right now what is happening in Gaza, I can't, I just, I can't go on every single day seeing this," she says. "I don't associate myself with what's happening."

I wonder what it must feel like. It must take great courage, to dissociate so fully, and under such difficult circumstances.

Back when I was in Egypt, in the fall of 2012, I got into an argument with an acquaintance of mine. He was then a young rising star in the ranks of the military. Egyptians, he said, aren't ready for democracy. They need stability, the kind only a disciplined, capable entity like the military can provide. Otherwise, he argued, you end up with Islamists, terrorists, people who'd cut your head off if you don't believe exactly what they believe. Is that what you want?

Much like the insidious foreign plot, the notion that people simply aren't prepared for democracy is a fundamental rhetorical tool of failing regimes. Whatever this is might feel oppressive, the argument goes, but you have no idea how much worse abandoning this way of doing things will be.

It's an odd thing to watch a variant of this argument take root in the West. There's immense persuasive power to the notion that the only alternative to mainstream Democratic politics is fascistic Republicanism. Who are Muslim Americans going to turn to? The Arab authoritarians from whom so many of them escaped? China, where Muslims are regularly thrown into concentration camps? Russia, where political opponents are assassinated as a matter of course?

It's a kind of thinking predicated on the implicit belief that, for certain people, the only choice is between negations of varying severity. *The system does not work for you, was never intended to work for you, but as an act of magnanimity on our part, you may choose the degree to which it works against you.*

While any liberal politician who succumbs to the lure of this framing may benefit in the short term, there is an inevitable and deeply unpleasant terminus waiting. Eventually, the calculus becomes, on pragmatic terms, clear. How much worse can some hypothetical oppression be compared to the current, very real one, which has the additional indignity of being propped up politically and financially by the same Free World whose leaders simultaneously give impassioned speeches about their support for democracy? If both outcomes entail injury, why should anyone opt for the one that adds insult too?

For some, even a hint of self-interest already produces these kinds of results—consider the gaggle of world-famous sports stars who've happily sided with murderous regimes such as that of Saudi Arabia, helping whitewash the government's image in exchange for not much more than money. For others, the bar is much, much higher. But the moral prohibition on siding with any administration that endorses genocide will force a different flavor of the exact same logic that centrist liberalism has depended on for so long: hold your nose and align with the least worst thing. Only the least worst thing will no longer be the mild, ethics-agnostic emptiness of modern Western liberalism, nor will it be the multitude of barbaric authoritarians and their secret prisons. It will be communal solidarity, or else nothing, a walking away from all of this. Countless otherwise pragmatic people who would in any other circumstance choose liberalism by default will instead decide none of this is worth the damage to one's soul. They will instead support no one, vote for no one, wash their hands of any ordering of the world that results in choices no better than this. And the obvious centrist refrain—*But do you want the deranged right wing to win?*—should, after even a moment of self-reflection, yield to a far more important question: How empty does your message have to be for a deranged right wing to even have a chance of winning? Of all the epitaphs that may one day be written on the gravestone of Western liberalism, the most damning is this: *Faced off against a nihilistic, endlessly cruel manifestation of conservatism, and somehow managed to make it close.*

Asked whether she still supports Joe Biden after these months of U.S.-approved calamity, Alexandria Ocasio-Cortez says she does. "I think sometimes people want electoral politics to be . . . we overly identify with . . . it's like, if you vote for someone they have to be the embodiment of you."

I don't want someone who's an embodiment of me. An embodiment of me doesn't stand a chance in hell. When a Muslim congressman goes on a morning show in 2015 and says Trump might win, he's almost laughed off the set by the other pundits. When a Palestinian American congresswoman calls for Palestine to be free, she's censured—her colleagues, however, are free to call for the eradication of Palestinians without consequence. Even candidates who are remotely like me are told by huge swaths of the United States, time and time again: You are not the same, the rules for you are not the same, what you have to say is lesser. No, I don't want a candidate who's the embodiment of me. I want a candidate who doesn't bankroll genocide. Failing that, I want the superhuman powers of dissociation that even the Democratic Party's progressive vanguard seem able, in a pinch, to conjure.

One day the killing will be over, either because the oppressed will have their liberation or because there will be so few left to kill. We will be expected to forget any of it ever happened, to acknowledge it if need be but only in harmless, perfunctory ways. Many of us will, if only as a kind of psychological self-defense. So much lives and dies by the grace of endless forgetting.

But so many will remember. We say that, sometimes, when it's our children killed: *Remember*. And it may seem now like it's someone else's children, but there's no such thing as someone else's children. The problem with fixating on the abyss into which one's opponent has descended while simultaneously digging one's own is that, eventually, it gets too dark to tell the difference.

CHAPTER EIGHT

FEAR

The rainwater is the property of the state. Certain roads are for some but not others. Certain buses are for some but not others. Cinnamon is fine and can be brought in, cardamom is a security threat and cannot. The list of prohibited items changes according to the whims of those enforcing it—dried fruit, cattle, chocolate. At the checkpoints some pass, others are made to wait hours and hours, just for the hell of it, just as a reminder. A woman miscarries, waiting. A cancer patient dies, waiting. An area is designated safe, then bombed. A soldier shoots a teenage girl seventeen times and is found not guilty. Life goes on, for some but not others.

Los Angeles, 2018:

It had been a long book tour. I'd spent the better part of a year, on and off, doing events for anemic audiences all over Europe and North America. (The low point comes in a scented-candles-and-trinkets store in Tampa that also occasionally sells books. Three people show up, one of whom had intended to come to a different author's event but got the date wrong, and is now too embarrassed to leave.) The cities begin to bleed together, and even LA seems like just another amalgam of downtown hotel and odd-smelling airport shuttle. I'm in town for an event, and afterward I rush back to the hotel to log on to a virtual meeting with a book club based in Egypt.

I was told once—sincerely, I think—that my novels make good book club fodder because the people who dislike them really hate them, and so at least there's something to talk about. (Sometimes you get these books everyone likes, this woman said, and it's just so boring.) Occasionally I'd get yelled at, as I did once at a faculty event at a university in Toronto, where one professor accused me of trying to get my readers to side with terrorists. But for the most part, people are kind.

I start to keep a list of frequently asked questions at these events. The year before my novel was published, in an attempt to make friends in Portland, I'd signed up for a stand-up comedy class. Among the instructor's most practical pieces of advice was to always have a solid five in your back pocket—a well-tested five-minute set of jokes you can always fall back on in a pinch. I begin creating my own solid five—answers to the questions I get most often. You can't make up a different origin story every time you're asked to explain why you started writing the novel, so best to polish the real one into something remotely interesting.

Among book clubs especially, I find one of the questions I get most often about *American War* has to do with a section in the middle of the novel set in a displaced-person's camp along the Mississippi-Alabama border, a place called Camp Patience. The section culminates in a massacre. Repeatedly I'm asked why I had to make those scenes so brutal. In response, I try to explain that much of the section references the 1982 massacre at Sabra and Shatila, Palestinian refugee camps in Lebanon (*sabr* is the Arabic word for "patience"). The events, the lines of dialogue, the brutality, it's all as described in the witness testimony of the actual event.

And then that night in Los Angeles, as I ready my usual list of answers for the most frequently asked questions, one of the members of the Egyptian book club—for whom Sabra and Shatila are not some faraway place—asks me something different.

If that scene is based on Sabra, she says, why did you tone it down so much?

●

Early in 2024, around the same time the genocide case was brought before the International Court of Justice, an ice storm hits Oregon. Much of the state grinds to a halt. I was out on the coast at the time, teaching at a residency in Seaside, a little tourist town that hibernates between summers, the arcades and saltwater taffy emporiums mostly vacant. The fastest routes between Seaside and Portland pass over the mountains, but for days after the storm the asphalt turned to glass; the drive home, normally ninety minutes, took me four hours. It was white-knuckle the whole way.

129

A couple of days later, with the ice still hanging like little pendants from the leaves, a burst of wind uprooted a forty-foot tree in our backyard. When it came down, diagonally across our yard, it made a sound that reminded me of the big guns in Afghanistan, of air pushed violently outward.

When dawn broke, we went outside to inspect the damage. Most of the back deck fencing was crushed, as was part of the deck itself. The furthest tip of the crown had just missed the roof of the small unit I use as my writing room. All in all, we got very, very lucky.

Yet for a week afterward, this feeling of nausea trailed me through the days. Some twelve hours before that tree came down, my daughter and her best friend had a playdate at our house, during much of which they ran around on the deck that now lies in ruins. I keep imagining the scene of that tree falling just a few hours earlier, what would have happened.

It's embarrassing, self-centered. For months now I have been reading stories and seeing pictures and watching footage of the most horrendous things that can happen to a child, to anyone. And yet there passes this strange sick period where I keep thinking about some hypothetical catastrophe, because no matter how hypothetical it may be, the person to whom it could have happened is mine.

Fear obscures the necessity of its causing. No one has ever been unjustifiably afraid, not in their own mind. An old college professor of mine once said a fundamental tenet of logic theory is that, from a false premise, any implication is true. Fear functions this way, too, causes the whole of the world to flower in limitless, terrible possibility.

It has always been this way—not just in this moment, this culmination of so many previous moments, but as a precondition of existence within a system whose currency of justification is fear. And it is a currency. The exchange rate is very real.

I fear, for example, large flags of the Western world, in almost any context. When I see them hanging off the backs of pickup trucks anywhere in the United States, I have an instinctual negative reaction. In Canada, over the last few years, as a pale imitation of the U.S.'s right wing has taken over more of the public sphere, I've come to develop the same reaction (despite the well-worn trope of slapping a Canadian flag on your luggage when traveling abroad as a preemptive declaration of niceness). The flags of France and the United Kingdom I can't help but imagine looming over the homes and neighborhoods and nations of my ancestors in the Arab world. (Though I realize, as I write this, that I have no similar fear of Arab nations' flags. Not a single one, including that of the country of my birth, induces any emotion at all, positive or negative.)

Not only is this fear irrational, it is largely untested. I have never tried to pull up beside one of those large trucks to ask the driver what he thinks of people like me. But much like the fear that arrives, invariably, whenever I have to pass through a border crossing, it isn't the rationality or evidence of the fear that matters, but rather its purchasing power. My fear, on account of who I am and what place I occupy in the West, buys me nothing. Less than nothing—the majority response I expect from admitting my wariness of large American flags on the backs of pickup trucks isn't some nuanced discussion about the fermentable nature of patriotism, but rather the insinuation that this isn't fear at all, but hatred, ungratefulness: *Well, leave, then. You don't like it? Leave.*

My fear buys nothing. I expect it to buy nothing. In this case, I *want* it to buy nothing—who cares how I feel about flags? And yet, I know other people's fear—as irrational as mine, more irrational than mine—buys everything. It moves armies, obliterates thousands. As with rage, there is an invisible force to fear, a gravity. I can no more push my fear upward into another echelon of privilege than those above me can help but let theirs fall, with terrible force, onto the lives of those below.

In early February 2024, as the slaughter in Gaza continues, I watch U.S. politicians argue over a domestic immigration bill that would ramp up enforcement, impose emergency powers to deport migrants before they can apply for asylum, and generally overhaul some of the systems by which people are allowed to come to and live in the United States. Much of the political debate returns, repeatedly, to the question of whether the bill is sufficiently tough. Its toughness cannot be overstated, because the people on whom it is going to be tough—the fear of them, of a purity they might dilute—is its own justification. These same people against whom it is acceptable to exact virtually any kind of state violence, from the snatching away of their children to letting them drown in plain sight, must become the living, flowering product of unlimited fear.

Around the same time Democrats and Republicans argue over the bill, *New York Times* columnist Thomas Friedman writes a piece comparing Iran, the nation of more than 87 million, to a wasp. What laces the entire racist, nonsensical premise is fear. Everyone knows, instinctively, the recoil the sight of a wasp induces. But fear is no end in itself: its function here is to allow for the abdication of restraint—nobody has ever been blamed for wanting to swat a wasp. It might have stung.

(It almost goes without saying that to exist in the West as an Arab, a Muslim, a Persian, or anyone who might be mistaken for these is to have to accept Friedman's trite invective or else be accused of hysteria. After all, the argument goes, what he is doing is something much more high-minded than simply comparing entire groups of people to insects—quite literally a tactic some of the most murderous regimes in history used to justify the liquidation of millions, including in Rwanda, where the instruction to kill Tutsi "cockroaches" preceded a genocide. No, what Friedman is really engaged in is a precise autopsy by analogy, explaining to us his heightened understanding of geopolitics by means of clever reverse anthropomorphism, in which the United States is a lion trying to kill a wasp in a jungle, for some reason, and Israeli prime minister Benjamin Netanyahu is a lemur. It simply can't be that one of the two or three most high-profile columnists in the United States, employed by the country's newspaper of record and a recipient of journalism's highest honor—a man who at times in his career has been capable of excellent reporting—has done a monumentally bad job. And so it must be that the people upset at the smearing of entire regions of the world as parasitic insects are the ones who are too sensitive, too hyperbolic, and must never be allowed to sully the public sphere with such simplistic concerns.)

By the time Friedman's column runs, somewhere between 12,000 and 13,000 Palestinian children are dead, killed by a military that, be it answerable to a lemur or financed by an aging lion or whatever the analogy hallucinates, plainly exists outside the orbit of Western fear. It is not, in any meaningful sense, a matter of obliviousness. Most anyone remotely informed has by now either seen the mountain of evidence that lays bare the scale of the carnage or has actively chosen to look away from it. Either way, they know what this is.

Near the end of February, Israeli soldiers open fire on Palestinians lined up for food aid, killing more than a hundred. The Gaza Health Ministry reports another six have died of malnutrition.

But these deaths are of something foreign, and so cannot be the subject of fear. Such things can be discussed in terms of strategy—*Will the wholesale murder of tens of thousands of kids prove a tactical blunder? Is the child who had to bury every member of his family now a future threat? Will Hamas benefit?*— but the violence that might otherwise inspire true fear is ultimately happening to an insect, and what fool gives credence to an insect's thoughts on its own swatting?

■

In June 2006, a few days after I was hired full-time as a general assignment reporter, police across Ontario instigated one of the biggest terrorism arrests in Canadian history. The case, dubbed the "Toronto 18" on account of the initial number of suspects, was easily the most sensational piece of news in the country for the better part of two years. It began with police raids in several Ontario cities. Most of the people arrested were young men, some of whom were in the middle of transferring what they thought were the chemical components of a bomb. The case would continue through years of legal proceedings and, eventually, lead to the conviction of some of the suspects. It was a massive story, and my newspaper, thanks in part to a last-minute decision by one of the senior editors on the night of the first raids to bury the article on page A2, was badly beat by its competitors. The following Monday, our editor in chief called all the staff in the paper's Toronto headquarters to a meeting in the second-floor newsroom. He was furious.

To the best of my knowledge, there were only two members of the editorial staff at the time who had any personal experience with Islam, the Middle East, or generally any facet of the identities of the accused—myself and Kamal Al-Solaylee, who was then the paper's theater critic. We were dispatched to interview friends and family of the suspects, to visit the mosques they frequented, to get details of their lives. Within a few days, Kamal had (rightly) found a way to abandon this beat to which he had been so artificially assigned. I worked on the story, and almost nothing else, for the next two years. I won awards, became indispensable.

As with all such cases, the weight of the word "terrorism" torqued what would otherwise have been a regular crime story in all the most predictable ways. When my colleague and I tried to interview one of the suspects in prison, an official at that prison wrote to our editor to warn him he had terrorist sympathizers on the payroll. When I got my hands on internal documents showing how intensely Canada's Public Safety ministry tried to manage the media around the case, one of the first comments from a reader on the story was, *I don't trust any story about terrorism written by a guy named Omar.* Eventually, some of the eighteen suspects—the ones who'd acted as ringleaders, who'd tried to build detonators using instructional videos on the Internet—would see serious prison time. Others who, it became clear as the evidence came to light, were obviously young and stupid and desperate to be taken in by any social grouping, would be given a slap on the wrist. The initial high drama faded, as it always does, and over the next couple of years the Toronto 18 case became what it always was: another crime story.

But there is, from the earliest days of my reporting on that case, a detail that has always stayed with me. I was interviewing a source who had known several of the suspects well. He told me about a night, not long before the police raids, when one of the older suspects took one of the younger ones out to the woods north of Toronto.

The man had been mentoring the boy. On this night, the boy didn't know why they were headed out to the middle of nowhere. They parked on the side of the road and marched in near-pitch-dark to a place in the woods where the older man had come previously and dug a hole in the ground. A grave.

The older man gave the younger one a simple directive: If you don't do what we've been planning, if you don't follow through, this is where you end up, forever. Not in paradise, but in the ground, eaten by worms, forever.

I laughed when I first heard the story. The sheer absurdity of taking a teenager out to the forest in the dead of night for this sad little piece of melodrama, this performance that couldn't have possibly had any impact.

It wouldn't have, my source said, if this was the opening gambit. But the grave in the woods was instead the culmination of years of slow, painstaking work—work that began when the two met, and the older man showed the younger one pictures of mutilated corpses and said: Hey, brother, have you seen what's being done to your brothers and sisters in Kashmir? In Bosnia? In Palestine?

We don't like to talk about these things. We prefer our monsters materialized, not made.

In my adult life, which began around the time of the September 11 attacks, there has been no greater totem of fear in the Western world than the terrorist. So overwhelming is this construction that not only has it justified without question or consequence one of the largest killing sprees in modern history, but has imposed onto entire swaths of people a binary existence. Are you, as someone who looks like those people who blow themselves up, for or against this? Will you condemn it, condemn it ceaselessly and no matter how unrelated to your existence it may be? Are you one of the bad ones who hate us, or one of the good ones who will tell on the ones who hate us? Should you be caught in the crossfire of our efforts to weed out the bad people, will you understand we had no choice but to do this? What is your relationship with the limitless violence of which you have always been capable in our minds?

One of the most damaging, longest-lasting consequences of the War on Terror years is an utter obliteration of the obvious moral case for nonviolence. The argument that violence in any form debases us and marks the instant failure of all involved is much more difficult to make when the state regularly engages in or approves of wholesale violence against civilians and combatants alike. Instead, the case for nonviolence becomes, in the ugliest way, pragmatic: the state wants violence, because in that playing field it maintains every advantage, from bigger guns to total immunity to the privilege of perpetual victimhood.

Once, many years ago, I sat in on a court case in Ottawa where lawyers argued at length about the definition of "terrorism." In most Western contexts, this definition boils down to violence in pursuit of political goals. The debate eventually migrated to a hypothetical situation in which someone bombs a lemonade stand with the purpose of scaring people away from lemonade stands, on account of the bomber's distaste for lemons. It was a somewhat absurd half hour, but instructive to the extent that everyone involved seemed aware, in some sense, that "terrorism" as a designation was of no value to the state without at least a certain degree of diaphanousness. After two decades of destruction in Iraq and Afghanistan laundered through the silencing power of the term, it is tempting to make the argument that "terrorism" as a societal designation (meaning something that goes beyond the realm of legal terminology and into the realm of what we are willing to allow our societies to do and to become) is applied almost exclusively to Brown people. When a white man kills dozens of people in a concert or a synagogue or a school, it's a crime. A hate crime, sometimes. But terrorism requires a distance between state and perpetrator wide enough to fit a different kind of fear. The kind of fear that justifies the creation of entirely new laws, new modes of detention, new apparatuses of surveillance, anything, anything at all.

Maybe this extreme reluctance to acknowledge, let alone study, the kaleidoscopic pathology of terror isn't just driven by the oft-stated fear that to try to understand something is inseparable from pledging allegiance to it. Maybe the real fear is that, when one begins to consider the root systems of small-scale, sometimes state-supported, but often stateless evil, there's an obligation to apply the same rigor to the large-scale machinery of imperial evil. And in doing so, one might find that what drives and absolves the state of so much evil isn't the fear that not doing so will allow some terrorist to destroy the fabric of free society. But rather that the evil itself is necessary to the system it protects. That in the end there is no international rules-based order, no universal human rights, no equal justice for all, simply fleeting arrangements of convenience in which any amount of human collateral is deemed acceptable so long as it works in the empire's interest.

In reality, when it's convenient, liberals are well versed in every facet of fear, and the application of all it justifies. When it's the most powerful nation on earth conducting a decades-long campaign of retaliative obliteration against multiple countries (one of which had precisely nothing to do with the inciting incident), leaving upward of a million civilians dead, revenge becomes a temporarily useful virtue. When it's a herder on the other side of the planet burning an American flag after a drone operator in an Idaho strip mall mistook his children for terrorists, revenge becomes grotesque, the irredeemable realm of savages.

Because imagine what this man might do. Imagine the dark violence of which he might be capable, in the grip of such rage. This man, this *idea* of a man. He might feed on his hatred and after feeding he might feed others, create a movement, take over a nation, even. And then, and then, and then— who's to say?—conduct a decades-long campaign of retaliative obliteration against multiple countries. Can you imagine that? Can you imagine anything else?

In early February 2024, *The Wall Street Journal* publishes an opinion piece titled "Welcome to Dearborn, America's Jihad Capital."

Dearborn is a city in Michigan. It has probably the highest per capita Arab population of any metropolitan area in the United States. It seems pointless to note that the few times I've visited Dearborn, I was treated with more warmth and hospitality than almost anywhere else in this country.

As with Friedman's Animal Planet cosplay, the *Wall Street Journal* piece doesn't really matter as anything other than a celebration of agency. *Look what I can say about these people; look how far beneath me they are.* If anyone actually believed that Dearborn, or anywhere else in this country, was a "jihad capital," whatever that may mean, wouldn't the appropriate response be a military one? Isn't that what this country does to jihadists as a matter of course? So why not wipe Dearborn off the map, bomb it to oblivion? Because the point is not the violence. Violence comes later, most often at the hands of someone who reads enough of these pieces and decides to act explicitly on what is only implicitly implied. The point, the fundamental prerequisite, is to say: Against those people, those lesser people, anything can be justifiably done. The point is to flaunt permission.

Am I allowed to be afraid of this? And if so, what is the purchasing power of my fear?

I went to see Bill Clinton give a speech once, in Toronto, years after his presidency ended. When public figures of a certain stature run out their time in office, there's almost always a lucrative second career waiting in the form of speech giving. In this case, it was part of one of those seminars with titles like "Unleash Your Potential" or "A Day with Greatness" or "How to Master the Inner You." Of course the convention center hall on Front Street was full. People dressed up in their Sunday best and came out to hear this man who'd stamped his name on history deliver what turned out to be complete porridge. I assume by that point he could have recited most of it in his sleep.

As a lot of former presidents like to do, he eventually meandered onto the topic people in this part of the world like to call the Middle East peace process. Its failure, he argued in passing, wasn't a failure of Israeli compromise or intent, but rather one of Palestinian imagination. What this particular bromide is intended to mean, when Western officials trot it out time and time again, is that one party in these proceedings got a little too big for its britches, and if these perpetually angry people only understood the generosity with which they were being treated, they would not be in this mess. Anyone who has ever been forced to contend with the empire's footprint knows this argument by heart. *We treat you so much better than we have to; why are you so angry? Why did you make us do this to you?*

Where is the Palestinian Martin Luther King? I've heard said on more than one occasion, never accompanied by any self-reflection as to what kind of society necessitates a man like that, nor what that society ultimately did to him before his posthumous veneration. The implicit accusation is that certain people are incapable of responding to their mistreatment with grace, with patience, with love, and that this incapacity, not any external injustice, is responsible for the misery inflicted upon them.

But Palestinians do respond overwhelmingly with love. Just as the Indigenous populations of an entire hemisphere, subjected to the largest genocide in human history, responded overwhelmingly with love. Just as the Black communities in much of the United States, a country that quite simply would not exist in its current form were it not for the theft of their labor, responded overwhelmingly with love. Just as every people everywhere deemed acceptable collateral in service of the empire's interest responded overwhelmingly with love. Today I watched footage of a man kissing his son's foot as he buried the body so torn apart by the missiles that the foot was one of the only pieces the father could find in the rubble. Tell me this man doesn't know love, hasn't been made to know it in a way no human being should.

Except it is a love that cannot be acknowledged by the empire, because it is a people's love for one another. Anyone who has dragged a relative out from under the wreckage of a bombed building, who has held a friend bleeding to death in the street while the officer who pulled the trigger looks on, who has watched their water poisoned, their land burned, their communities starved, is intimately well versed in love. But in the eyes of the empire such a thing can never be called love, because the directive was never in the first place, *Love,* but rather, *Love me. In spite of it all, love me.*

In New York City, Joe Biden is met by Jewish protesters. It has become an almost everyday occurrence now, this resistance. There's a ham-fisted reaction on the part of the White House, the entire Democratic establishment, that seems to betray a genuine shock at this expression of moral solidarity among peoples. It's like watching someone get cursed out in a language they can't speak.

It's not surprising, I don't think, that in the midst of this indiscriminate killing, many of the Westerners doing the most active work in opposing genocide are Jews. Here is love born of pain, of the past century's most horrific crime, love of one's own spread outward into love of another. Whatever the empire is, it has no idea what to do with this kind of love, which adheres neither to the empire's own central principle of self-interest nor to the adjoining principle that solidarity is only with one's own, that love for one's people may never become love for another.

I happen to be in New York City the same time as the president, meeting with my publisher about the manuscript that will become this book. I ask one of my editors to tell me honestly if she thinks the publication will cause her and her colleagues trouble beyond the bounds of what can be usually expected from an overtly political book. She says she doesn't think so, in large part because the soonest this book could go out into the world is the following year, and the situation will almost certainly be different then.

I want to believe it. A month earlier, while I was conducting an interview for a podcast, my guest brings up the bombing in Gaza. Later, during editing, one of my producers leaves a note on the interview transcript: "flagging that I hope this is not still going to go on in March when this episode is released." When a friend of mine who runs a large literary festival calls up to discuss how to address the killings when the festival next takes place in the fall, we find that both of us are no longer even paying lip service that any of this will be "over" anytime soon, any more than it "began" the previous October.

A couple of days after the president's visit to New York, Israel begins a major incursion into Rafah, a city on the southernmost edge of Gaza where more than a million people have been sheltering and beyond which there is only expulsion into the Sinai desert. What frightens me about my publisher's argument that things will be different next year isn't that I don't believe her; it's that I do.

But that too is a useless fear. It buys nothing.

■

In the summer of 2021, I took my U.S. citizenship exam. The test is administered in a federal building on the northwest side of downtown Portland. I took a number, waited a while, and was called into a small office by a large, stern-faced officer who I'd later learn had migrated here himself from Austria.

The basics of every citizenship exam are the same. There's an English-language test, a civics/history quiz, and a rapid-fire set of questions about whether the applicant has ever engaged in human trafficking, kept someone from practicing their religion, or served in a foreign army, among other transgressions. For months, my wife and I spent our evenings preparing. When the day comes, I find myself as nervous as I thought I'd be. There's a kind of anxiety that kicks in whenever one has to submit to the whims of a system that can alter the trajectory of one's life. A sense that things only have to go wrong once.

I nod. I smile. I pass the language and civics tests; I say truthfully that I have never been involved in any way with genocide. A few weeks later, I become a citizen of the United States.

Immigrants are supposed to be grateful. The narrative arc of immigration, in which one flees their own failing society to come to a better place, a country that was under no obligation to accept them but did, demands perpetual gratitude. And it exists, this gratitude, but the narrative makes no room for the many shapes it comes in, its many less straightforward forms. I harbor no ill will toward the immigrant who waves the miniature flag on the sides of the Independence Day parade, who says honestly and plainly: I love this country. But nor do I judge the immigrant who is as emotionless and pragmatic about the nation-state as the people who run that nation-state are so regularly emotionless and pragmatic about immigrants, who says honestly and plainly: I don't love this country, don't love any country, patriotism being the property of an entirely different kind of life than luck has given me; I live here because it will always be safer to live on the launching side of the missiles. I live here because I am afraid.

On the second weekend of February 2024, the decomposing body of five-year-old Hind Rajab, whom the Israeli military murdered, is found in a car with her family, next to a burned-out ambulance that was dispatched to rescue her. Later, an independent investigation will find 355 bullet holes in the car Hind was in. But early on, the story is reported in multiple media outlets as though it were a missing-person's case, as though this child simply walked out of sight and then walked straight out of this life.

She had called for help. She had picked up a phone and begged for help. She cried, said she'd wet herself. She was five years old.

What is the word for what she felt? Because on the other side of the planet countless people cheering on this liquidation will wake up and say that they too are afraid. But if these are equal and offsetting fears then the word means nothing. As does any system, any way of living, that abides it.

A chasm has developed, these last few months, one of many but one that cannot be bridged. On one side is a portion of society that fears nothing more than the discontinuation of normalcy. That believes, regardless of what horror each new day brings, what matters most is to live as one had lived before, answering emails and meeting deadlines and maintaining productivity. On the other is that portion which, having witnessed the horror, is simply unable to continue as before. How does one live, hearing the screams, bearing witness to the bodies? How does anything else matter? The fear of some comfort disappearing collides with a different fear—a fear that any society whose functioning demands one ignore carnage of this scale for the sake of artificial normalcy is by definition sociopathic. Often, I watch discussions on social media in which someone asks: What radicalized you? In response, others will point to various moments of mass violence at the hands of the state, blatant cases of injustice, moments such as this one where it becomes clear there exists a massive gap between the empty statements of the powerful in support of justice and the application of actual justice. But the word "radicalize" feels wrong, seems to imply an element of extremism, as though rage at this kind of blatant hypocrisy is the abnormal thing, when what is plainly abnormal is to accept it.

In Toronto, a protest marches downtown, along University Avenue, one of the city's most iconic streets. Someone climbs up the scaffolding outside Mount Sinai Hospital, waves a Palestinian flag. Within a day, both the prime minister of Canada and the mayor of Toronto, along with several more of the country's political leaders, issue statements of condemnation, accusing the protesters of anti-Semitism and making it clear that hospitals are sacred sites, sites of healing. Maybe the protesters were raging anti-Semites, and for some reason decided the most effective expression of their hatred was to dress up in Spider-Man costumes and climb scaffolding outside a hospital.

None of these same politicians have issued any condemnation of the obliteration of Gaza's hospitals, which seemingly in the Western conception are not sites of healing, not sites at all. The damage this does has been glaring for months now, in the growing count of murdered doctors and patients and civilians seeking refuge in the non-hospitals of the non-world.

Near the grounds of Al-Shifa Hospital in Gaza, in the days after an Israeli siege, mass graves are discovered, the bodies in them bound with zip ties.

I want to live in a world where the worst thing imaginable is a protest nearing a hospital. I want the narcotic capacity to unsee mangled bodies, surgeons sniped in their operating room, a handcuffed prisoner ordered into a hospital to tell everyone to leave and then, on his return outside, executed—so that I too might calibrate my condemnations accordingly. It would be good to live in that world.

In reality, it doesn't much matter what or how vigorously I condemn. I am of an ethnicity and a religion and a place in the caste ordering of the Western world for which there exists no such thing as enough condemnation. This is what we are to do, always and to the exclusion of all else: condemn, apologize for, retreat into silence about any atrocity committed by anyone other than those to whom we are perpetually assumed allegiant. It is not sufficient to say I despise Hamas for the same reasons I despise almost every single governing entity in the Middle East—entities obsessed with violence as an ethos, brutal in their treatment of minority groups who in their view should not exist, and self-decreed to be the true protectors of an entire religion.

A very odd thing, to be deemed a potential agent of terrible violence and also be expected to offer unending deference. Along the axis of fear and possibility, some people are permanently assigned the negative quadrant, defined not by the horror of what might be done to them, but of what they might do.

There exists no other remotely plausible explanation for a moral worldview in which what a protester might hypothetically do to a hospital deserves the strongest condemnation, while what a military does—has done—to multiple hospitals deserves none.

Colonialism demands history begin past the point of colonization precisely because, under those narrative conditions, the colonist's every action is necessarily one of self-defense. The story begins not when the wagons arrive, but only after they are circled. In this telling, fear is the exclusive property of only one people, and the notion that the occupied might fear the doing of their occupier is as fantastical as the notion that barbarians might be afraid of the gate. Any population on whom this asymmetry is imposed will always be the instigators, the cause of what is and, simultaneously, the justification for what will be. The savage outside does, the civilized center must respond.

How does one finish the sentence: "It is unfortunate that tens of thousands of children are dead, but . . ."

Ignore for a moment that the number is an approximation. Ignore the many more children mutilated, orphaned, left to scream under the rubble. Ignore the construction of the sentence itself, its dark similarities to the language of every abuser—*You made me do this*. Ignore all of this and think about how you would finish this sentence that has now been uttered in one form or another by so many otherwise deeply empathetic Western liberals. How to finish it and still be able to sleep at night.

Surely, many people have, and their answers might relate to terrorists or revenge or an all-encompassing right to self-defense. But trimmed to its most basic language, every proposed conclusion to that sentence is some variant of the same basic thesis: *They would have killed more of ours.*

What does unlimited fear cost? What will sate it?

In February 2024 I go give a talk at a private school on the East Coast. It's a quintessential New England private school, the school and faculty overwhelmingly white, the annual tuition breathtaking. I had been invited almost a year earlier, and when I arrive, I try to get a sense from my host of how nervous she and everyone else here have become about this event. She assures me everything's fine—they have already touched base with the school's Jewish students' groups, and plan to have a debrief the day after my talk, to make sure everyone's all right.

Later that day, I'm invited to an assembly in the school chapel. After the singing of hymns, one of the senior administrators tells the audience that another swastika has been found on campus. This time it's in a place where there is security camera coverage, and that they will find whoever has been doing this.

That evening, I give my talk. The audience is kind. I don't think I scared anyone, but I'll never know for sure.

CHAPTER NINE

LEAVETAKING

In a hospital. In a refugee camp. In their beds. While making dinner for their children. While holding their siblings. While cycling. While playing on a beach. In a market. In an incubator. Struggling to breathe, under the rubble. While trying to drag a loved one from the middle of the road. While burying the dead. While scavenging for food. While selling vegetables. While swimming in the sea, trying to catch fish. While playing soccer. While waving a white flag. With their hands raised in surrender. With their hands tied. While running away. At a checkpoint. In a torture camp. In a safe zone. In a school. While delivering aid. While waiting on aid. While performing surgery. While sitting down in a chair. By drone, from the safety of great distance. Live on air. Away from sight.

Portland, 2024:

There's a half acre of wildwood behind our house in Oregon, full of blackberry brambles, mostly impassible. Sometime during the fourth or fifth or hundredth month of genocide, I find myself stomping a small path into the forest. I go off to a quiet place, away from the neighbors' sight lines, where I can be alone. Most days I'm alone in my office, the little space where I write, but it's in this room I bear witness to the dead. For reasons I'm not able to explain, I feel the need to walk to a different place to mourn them. Somewhere beautiful.

It's not a familiar reflex. The last time I remember openly weeping was in Cairo's Rabaa Mosque near the end of Ramadan in 2010, the morning we prayed over and then buried my father's body. Among the generation of Arab men who raised me, it's looked down upon. In the forest, all these years later, I find no catharsis in it, no sensation of any kind. It feels more like an immune response, something the body, faced with disease, just does.

More and more, daily life seems to invert. The very consequential work of figuring out taxes and filing stories and handing students their essays back becomes utterly trivial. When I'm offered a book deal, my friend asks how we're going to celebrate, and for a moment I genuinely believe he's joking. Spousal arguments, contract negotiations, deadlines—everything sheds its veneer of importance. The only thing that seems paramount is to spoil my kids.

I decline most professional invitations—events, assignments, panels where I know I'll be the token Brown guy. But then I'm invited to an awards ceremony in Los Angeles. Having just gone on a radio show a day earlier to berate other artists for not having the guts to use their acceptance speeches to call for an end to the genocide, I feel like a hypocrite if I don't go.

154

I stand in a ballroom amid hundreds of cheerful, celebratory people and it occurs to me I've lost the ability to be here. I have spent the entirety of my life stitching together costumes to make Westerners feel at ease in my presence—a massive internal compendium of cultural references and jokes and shorthand and all these alternate means of saying, *Don't worry, I'm not foreign, I'm like you*—and suddenly I've run out of things to wear. The defining emotion, as it has been for months, is bewilderment: What is wrong with me that I can't keep living as normal? What is wrong with all those people who can?

●

On Sunday, February 25, 2024, a man named Aaron Bushnell walked up to the gates of the Israeli embassy in Washington, D.C., and set himself on fire. His last words were, "Free Palestine."

In the moments before his death, Bushnell spoke more lucidly and with greater moral clarity than almost any Western politician. It is no small thing, to downplay the work of a man like that, a man whose passing leaves a gaping maw of grief not simply by virtue of his act but by the irrefutable fact that the world, in the span of that act, loses a rare voice unwavering in its orientation to justice.

And yet people try.

In no time and requiring no evidence at all, some of the same pundits whose tolerance for domestic protest has always been nonexistent will float the idea that Bushnell suffered

155

from mental illness. In the mindset of the modern centrist, where every societal act must be transactional, Occam's razor slices away any other explanation: You don't hurt yourself for the sake of someone else—you believe yourself capable of it in the abstract, to be sure, but only because that belief, too, is transactional, the reward being a superficial moral ablution. But to see someone—a soldier in the world's most powerful military—do this outside of the abstract, in service of very real principles and in honor of the very real dead and dying, presents to a vacuously liberal worldview the ethical equivalent of a division-by-zero error. The purpose, outcome, logic of such a thing, it's all undefined. Whoever does it must be misguided, insidious, or mentally ill. When in 2010 the Tunisian street vendor Mohamed Bouazizi set himself on fire in a protest now widely recognized as the instigating moment of the Arab Spring, a parade of the same pundits and politicians praised it as heroism of the highest order. *Look at what these noble people will do in pursuit of their own freedom.* But here the man at the center of the flames cannot be venerated from so safe a distance. He wears the uniform of the country he served, the country whose leadership funds the genocide he offers up his life to oppose. There is no transaction here.

Power absent ethics rests on an unshakable ability and desire to punish active resistance—to beat and arrest and try to ruin the lives of people who block freeways and set up encampments and confront lawmakers. But such power has no idea what to do against negative resistance, against someone who refuses to buy or attend or align, who simply says: I will not be part of this. Against the one who walks away.

■

In mid-February 2024, the United States once again vetoes a resolution calling for a ceasefire in Gaza. Most everyone sees it coming, and for all the rhetorical backlash afterward, nobody seriously believes the administration endorsing this genocide is going to suddenly participate in even a ventriloquism of concern. The image that once again graces most articles about the veto is of the U.S. ambassador to the United Nations, Linda Thomas-Greenfield, raising her hand. This is not the first time she has done this, sinking a ceasefire resolution on the grounds that it might jeopardize U.S. efforts to bring lasting peace to the region. As a matter of course, Western officials are generally untroubled when they say things like this, that a ceasefire resolution represents a greater threat to lasting peace than the ongoing obliteration of an entire people.

(There have been close to nine hundred UN General Assembly resolutions related to "the question of Palestine" in the past seventy-five years. Resolutions on the status of refugees, self-determination, independence, the right of return, condemnations, emergency sessions, demands, peace negotiations . . .)

Around the middle of my decade in journalism, I spent a year primarily as a political reporter. Between that beat and my frequent trips to Gitmo, I slowly built relationships with various Pentagon spokespeople. There are things you learn, immersed in this backworld of governance, that in hindsight might seem obvious but, witnessed up close, have about them the discomforting sense of the phantasmagoric. The elected politicians whose names and faces are ubiquitous features of the public sphere melt away into a hydra of hangers-on: people who will never run for office themselves, but have found their calling on the periphery of someone electable. Most every political system runs on the efforts of people such as these, people who do the driving and pick up the laundry and piece together the press statements without the slightest twinge of concern for what relationship, if any, those statements might have with reality.

I think about this entourage now, as I watch Ambassador Thomas-Greenfield at work. I imagine the driver and the town car that whisks her elsewhere. I imagine an office, a suite of offices, littered with assistants and secretaries and the living accoutrements of institutional power: coffee that appears by magic, missives dictated, the small annoyances of daily living taken care of by a fleet of underlings so that this person, this deeply important and yet instantly replaceable person, can go about the work of being ushered into a wide-open room to sit at a large curving desk ahead of a sign that reads UNITED STATES and raise her hand as instructed to veto a toothless resolution calling for an end to genocide.

I imagine the quiet insides of that town car, before and then after this person has followed the orders she must follow. I wonder whether, in that momentary silence, watching through the window as the scummy world of the everyday living floats by, deeply unimportant, this person might wonder, even briefly, if this is what she wanted for her life.

And then I watch an interview with a Palestinian child who is asked what she misses most and answers: Bread.

Negation—the power to turn away—is a dangerous thing, and the narrative changes wildly depending on who's doing it. When the administration trots out one of its officials to veto a ceasefire resolution or has some press secretary smugly spout nonanswers to questions about an ally's plainly spoken intent to commit atrocity, it is simply the way statecraft is practiced. But should individuals choose not to buy a product made by a company complicit in such atrocity, it is an act of economic terrorism. Whole swaths of the founding freedoms of the Western world must be temporarily set aside so as to pass laws prohibiting this kind of thing. (More than thirty-five U.S. states have passed laws either restricting the ability to boycott goods related to Israel or making it illegal for companies and individuals who do to work for or with the state.) When the world's wealthiest nations decide, on the flimsiest pretext, to cut funding to the one agency that stands between thousands of civilians and slow, hideous death by starvation, it is a prudent anti-terrorism measure. But when voters decide they cannot in good conscience participate in the reelection of anyone who allows this starvation to happen, they are branded rubes at best, if not potential enablers of a fascist takeover of

Western democracy. Because the individual cannot be allowed to walk away, cannot be afforded an all-encompassing right *not* to participate. Not when the entire system depends, in a very existential sense, on continued participation, on ever-increasing participation.

Daily we are told there is nothing better than this. Our graphics cards and loafers arrive at our doorsteps the same day we order them—what more is there to want? We hurtle from shock to shock, bubble to bubble, oriented in the direction of complete ecological collapse and a future mortgaged beyond any hope of repayment. Yet we are told the most frightening thing is not this building chaos, but rather the possibility that any other course might end in secret police and breadlines. Daily the entirety of the right-wing sphere and an alarming number of liberals fret about a generation of young people deluded into Marxism or some other ideological bogeyman. When students at the most prestigious universities in North America build encampments in solidarity with Palestine, it's difficult to believe the institutional response isn't colored by a sense of betrayal. These young people have been afforded entry into the heart of the system, with all the privileges that entails. That they should jettison such a privilege in favor of a people on the other side of the planet who are able to offer nothing in return—to an ideology fixated on self-interest, it must seem like an embrace of nihilism.

In reality, what is happening is the opposite of an embrace. It's a shoving aside of the present system, a system that makes it more and more clear there is no future, no community, for

this or any other generation to come. Only endless taking—
and if these young people must pay for it by forfeiting hope
or possibility or clean air or a livable planet, so be it. A system
more petulant and intransigent than any protester who ever
lived. A system that can only ever say: There is nothing better
than this.

■

I watch videos of the playwright Victor I. Cazares conducting
burial ceremonies for their HIV medication. In one, there's a
tart, simple intimacy to the act—the kneading of the earth, the
gentle placing of a wildflower on the grave. In another, there's a
pyre, a burning. In another, there's music, a smear of blood left
as a parting gift to the pill that helps keep the person parting
with it alive. In December 2023, Cazares goes on a medication
strike, refusing to take their pills until the New York Theatre
Workshop, with which Cazares is affiliated, calls for a ceasefire
and an end to the occupation of Palestine.

I know nothing about Cazares or the New York Theatre
Workshop. I have no idea what either the playwright or the
institution's wider politics are, beyond the details of the strike
itself—though I suspect the Workshop, like so many cultural
institutions, has come to the conclusion that celebrating
dangerous art is a self-glorifying thing to do in the abstract, not
so much in reality.

(All over the Western world, beginning with cultural
organizations but not ending there, a reckoning is underway. In

a moment of wanton bloodshed, the people who run festivals, awards, residencies, the entire spectrum of organizations intended to support artists and their work, are having to contend with the difference between penultimate consequences and ultimate ones. Money is a penultimate consequence. Participation is the ultimate consequence. I hardly know any literary organization that doesn't struggle with money, and losing donors is no small thing. Having to hold an awards ceremony or festival in a smaller venue for lack of resources isn't ideal. But losing the support of the very people without whom the award or festival would not exist is something else entirely.)

For months I've watched presidents and prime ministers balk at calling for a ceasefire that most of their electorate supports, for fear that trying to end a genocide might in some way prove politically disadvantageous. For months I've watched this utter moral emptiness, which in such plain, undisguised form often feels so much more insidious than active support of this horror. Now I watch a human being boycott the very insurance of their continued physical health.

These acts of overwhelming personal consequence shatter the brittle veneer of the world as a place of total self-interest. But even the smallest acts matter. A friend decides not to do a book club event after she's told by the organizers that all questions about Palestine will be removed preemptively. The writer Lana Bastašić terminates her contract with a German publishing house for not being vocal enough in opposing the genocide. The director Jonathan Glazer, accepting an Oscar on the biggest stage in the cultural world, uses the moment to renounce the hijacking of his religion for the purpose of mass killing. Countless artists, many of whom can barely make ends meet, turn away from prizes and fellowships and speaking engagements when it becomes clear the institutions running and funding these things aren't much more than a vehicle for some rich donor's nice evening out. Multiple Biden administration employees resign. While accepting an award for excellence, NYU nurse Hesen Jabr describes the killing in Gaza as a genocide—she's fired for it. The director of a literary organization I admire, acknowledging at the start of a reading that so much of what we do right now feels so pointless, returns still to the rallying cry issued by the Palestinian poet Rasha Abdulhadi: "Wherever you are, whatever sand you can throw on the gears of genocide, do it now. If it's a handful, throw it. If it's a fingernail full, scrape it out and throw. Get in the way however you can."

During the bad days, of which there are now almost nothing but, it is impossible to ignore that what waits, most often, on the other side of this sand-throwing is silence. One donates their speaking fees to a charity that attempts to get medical aid and food to starving children and there on the other side is only silence. One advises the director of a festival that any acknowledgment of the horror is better than none, knowing that what will almost certainly follow that acknowledgment is a silence or polite applause that becomes its own form of silence. No society in human history has ever donated or applauded its way out of a genocide.

But then to see a group of U.S. veterans at a memorial for Aaron Bushnell, at the site of his protest; to see hundreds of thousands marching, taking ground outside the constituency offices of their elected officials; to watch even the normally anonymous executives of weapons manufacturers face both active and negative resistance, students protesting at the factories and dockworkers refusing to load the missiles onto the ships—to see these things is to know the sand *is* sticking to the teeth. The gears *will* grind to a halt one day, and the silence that waits then, for those who commended this killing and for those who said nothing, will be of a far more burrowing kind. It will take the form of grandchildren who, when the subject comes up, will pretend not to know how their grandparents behaved, will awkwardly try to talk about anything else. It will take the form of previous statements quietly deleted, previous opinions abandoned and replaced with shiny new ones about how, yes, it was such a terrible thing that happened. And finally, it will take the form of a quiet unheard reckoning in the winter of life between the one who said nothing, did nothing, and their own soul. And there will be no words exchanged then, only a knowing.

In late February 2024 I talk to a friend of mine, a Palestinian Canadian author whose debut novel, rejected by many publishers, seems to have finally found a home. He says he still doubts whether it'll actually go out into the world. But he takes some solace in the likelihood that, by next year or the year after, it won't just be Gaza that's on fire, but the whole world, so what difference does it make what one book does? We laugh, but I can't mount much of a counterargument. I know when an Arab says things like this, there's a natural impulse to believe he's talking about some great violent retribution, but I know what my friend means. A world that shrugs at one kind of slaughter has developed a terrible immunity. No atrocity is too great to shrug away now, the muscles of indifference having been sufficiently conditioned.

I tell him I'm struggling between walking away from almost all my professional obligations—panels, juries, prize and fellowship announcements that suddenly appear stripped of any meaning at all—and a sense of not wanting to cede ground, wanting to be in the room.

Sure, he says, but it'll still be the same room.

Even walking away sometimes feels no more or less hollow than any other pragmatic solution to what should never have been a pragmatic issue. That it might work—as it did, finally, after the economic ostracization of apartheid South Africa— only reinforces that there was never any morality among those atop the empire's food chain, only a greed momentarily exploited. In the midst of the world's first livestreamed genocide, when plain before the eyes of anyone who cares to look are shown the most visceral details, one of the few things that inspires any real panic on the part of most Western power centers is the prospect of reduced shipping activity through the Red Sea. For the moment, whatever will bring an end to this killing is worth doing, but one cannot help but ask: If the system to which I am forced to appeal responds only to attacks on its self-interest, what is there to hope for but that the next glaringly obvious injustice just happens to not quite perfectly intersect with that self-interest? What is the ethical legitimacy of any system in which one has to hope the most privileged sliver of global society decides, in large enough numbers, that a sufficient number of children have been murdered to warrant choosing a different brand of couscous? That enough migrants have been caged or drowned to make a particular vacation spot unappealing? That the well-being of Congolese children outranks the desire for ever more powerful smartphones?

Active resistance—showing up to protests and speaking out and working to make change even at the smallest levels, the school boards and town councils—matters. Negative resistance—refusing to participate when the act of participation falls below one's moral threshold—matters. And yet there are days when both negative and active resistance feel pointless. A political system that won't restrict firearms even after a shooter massacres classrooms full of children, a system that shrugs when a regime murders and dismembers a journalist because that regime controls an inordinate amount of oil, a system that won't flinch at the images of starving babies when it has the power to save their lives—what manner of resistance can't such a system learn to abide? What use is any of it, what use?

But there *is* a use, always. The first is outward: every derailment of normalcy matters when what's becoming normal is a genocide. It doesn't take much: by the standards of Western normalcy, where the possibility of a missile landing on one's

house or a military sniper murdering one's children is so
implausible as to be indistinguishable from science fiction,
even minimal inconvenience is tantamount to apocalypse.
The second is inward: every small act of resistance trains
the muscle used to do it, in much the same way that turning
one's eyes from the horror strengthens that particular muscle,
readies it to ignore even greater horror to come. One builds
the muscle by walking away from the most minor things—
trivial consumables, the cultural work of monsters, the myriad
material fruits grown on stolen ground—and realizes in the
doing of these things that there is a wide spectrum of negative
resistance. Maybe it's not all that much trouble to avoid
ordering coffee and downloading apps and buying chocolate-
flavored hummus from companies that abide slaughter.

It is this realization that renders negative resistance most
terrifying to political and economic power—the simple fact
that, having taken these small steps, a person might decide
it was no great sacrifice, and might be willing to sacrifice
more, demand more. That having called for justice in one
instance, one might do it again and again, might call for a just
world. It is probably the case that most mainstream Western
politicians don't actually care one iota about Israelis or
Palestinians and, were the calculus of electoral self-interest to
shift, would happily back whatever position serves their own
interests best. But what about a population whose inability to
countenance genocide spreads outward, becomes an inability
to countenance what the same political systems do and will
always allow to happen to so much of the planet in the name of

endless extraction, endless *more*? Such a thing puts the entire ordering at risk.

■

When the Israeli military opens fire on starving civilians clambering for flour, *The Guardian* describes the killings as "food aid–related deaths." One struggles to imagine how food aid could do such a thing.

"As with many events in the war between Israel and Hamas," *The Economist* reports, "the facts are destined to remain fiercely contested."

It is destiny for facts to be fiercely contested.

To orient oneself in relation to this kind of equivocation as it exists in the West—where a genocide is a conflict of equals, and really who's to say what a sufficient number of dead civilians is, and it's all so complicated anyway—is to temporarily forget that most of the world sees this for what it is *right now*. This mandatory waiting period, in which the rest of the planet politely pleads with the West's power centers to bridge the gap between its lofty ideals and its bloodstained reality, to do anything at all, is not some natural phenomenon, but the defining feature of neoliberalism. What purer expression of power than to say: *I know. I know but will do nothing so long as this benefits me. Only later, when it ceases to benefit me, will I proclaim in great heaving sobs my grief that such a thing was ever allowed to happen. And you, all of you, even the dead in their graves, will indulge my obliviousness now and my*

repentance later because what affords me both is in the end not
some finely honed argument of logic or moral primacy but the
blunt barrel of a gun.

Once, in Portland, I was invited to an awards ceremony
honoring local businesses. One company received an award
for—I forget now: trailblazing? synergy? something, on
account of completing a particularly difficult job in Israel.
The company was a labor middleman, it specialized in getting
other corporations the workers they needed, and in this case,
at the last minute, the owners of a manufacturing plant decided
that no Palestinians would be allowed to work there. So the
labor supplier scrambled, but managed to source the workers
from somewhere in Eastern Europe. For this, they were being
presented with an award that night in Portland. The whole
room applauded.

It is not simply the case that, seeing this kind of thing
up close, one is made to contend with some new, terrible
degeneration of the West, a corruption of its ideals or stated
ethical orientation. It is that, upon seeing this, time and time
and time again—in beautifully catered awards ceremonies
celebrating apartheid, and in the killing fields of Gaza,
and in the blunt knowledge that the two are not all that
disconnected—one cannot help but realize that there has been
no degeneration, no corruption. That so far as the West stands
in historical reality, nothing has evolved, nothing has become
more enlightened, nothing has been learned. It has always been
this way.

And here it would be dishonest to look away from the anger such an indictment inevitably inspires—the voice that, affronted this way, responds: Fine, then, side with the broken, lesser world, side with the countries that can't pay their debts or keep their lights on or maintain even the semblance of civil society, side with the terrorists (you will always be said to side with the terrorists), side with, as the chief political instigator of our present moment put it, darkness against light—and don't come crying to us when we crush you.

Perhaps that is what this all comes to, in the end, some pathetic adherence to the idea that certain peoples simply need to be crushed. But whoever subscribes to this idea should at least have the spine to embrace it. To look upon the body of the little girl hanging from the wall, limbs severed by the force of the blast, and say: I'm fine with this, I am this. At least there'd be some measure of honesty in it.

■

This work of leaving, of aiming to challenge power on the field where it maintains the least glaring asymmetry, demands one answer the question: What are you willing to give up to alleviate someone else's suffering? It makes it impossible for one so engaged to not understand, with terrible clarity, that under the auspices of this machine, the prevailing answer echoing from the mouths of so many of one's own neighbors is: *Nothing at all.*

Beyond the obvious bad-faith efforts to preserve existing

power, one of the central arguments against walking away has always depended on the idea that doing so entails a certain kind of cynicism: How can you hope for anything to change if you won't participate in the work of changing it? How can you have any moral standing if you are so susceptible to abandoning hope?

It's a compelling position, or would be in anything like a justly ordered world. But within the confines of *this* world, one in which our political, institutional, and corporate leaders—people who could do something about this *right now*—simply feign concern at an ongoing genocide or actively cheer it on, it cannot be anything but the straightforward manifestation of an imaginative desert. The system, predicated on endless feeding, is unable to imagine anything outside itself, let alone forms of resistance to itself. Since all benefit under such a system is individualistic, it becomes equally impossible to imagine any benefit to an individual walking away from it—*What is to be gained? Some kind of moral cleanliness? Be serious.*

The obvious charge of hypocrisy looms over this work, always. Refrain from engaging with one organization because of its ties to a genocide but not the uncountable number of other organizations who do as well? Call for divestment from fossil fuel companies and yet still use electricity? Agitate for a better world in any way and yet continue to exist within it?

The purpose of this kind of accusation is never moral concern. To be accused of speaking too loudly about one injustice but not others by someone who doesn't care about any of them is to be told, simply, to keep quiet.

The imaginative obligation of progress is infinite. A person the system was never built to serve bears the responsibility of dreaming up a better one, and who can say how much better? So many progressive movements splinter this way. Power bends even a little, and for some that's good enough. Others want more. Still others want the entire system demolished. A person the system was built to serve bears no such responsibility, has no reason to imagine anything better.

But the notion that individuals who walk away might find common cause, might use that cause to build something that, if not entirely separate from the system, is at least not completely aligned with it, reads to the system—to *any* system of empire—as fantasy. For someone fortunate enough to be born wearing the boot, the capacity for mercy may well extend only to how hard one chooses to step on the neck. That anyone should take the shoe off entirely, walk from the site of the trampling, is unthinkable.

Or maybe it's not. Maybe the centers of power have always been cognizant of a very limited ability to punish or control those who refuse to participate. Negative resistance becomes, then, the only thing that truly terrifies an ordering of endless appetite. The machine swallows life and spits out convenience. If liberalism has finally decided it is safe enough to consider the Black people whose labor built the machine as human, and the Indigenous people whose obliteration made room for the machine as human, and maybe the distant foreigners who sew our clothes and solder our motherboards might be human, and the inconvenient occupied whose land and water might hold resources we implicitly know but cannot explicitly say would be so much better used in service of the civilized world might be human, and if even the natural world and its inhabitants deserve the rights of humans—well, what's left to feed the machine? What's left to manufacture convenience?

When push comes to shove, the state is completely fluent in the violent power of negation, of turning away. When the White House instructs its ambassador at the United Nations to veto a resolution, when a whole host of Western nations cut aid to the one agency trying most desperately to keep Palestinians from starving to death, when the president grieves over photos of dead babies he never saw but thinks nothing of thousands of very real dead children who in his mind are beneath mourning, there are no illusions on the part of anyone involved as to what these acts of severance are designed to achieve.

What will always flummox the state is the prospect of the individual—of many individuals—employing negation as a political tactic. What to do with someone who doesn't rush the podium, doesn't spit on the flag, doesn't do anything to ease the state's transition into the comfortable arena of violence? What to do with someone who says: *I will have no part of this,* when the entire functionality of the system is dependent on active participation? Forced into this kind of space, power becomes enraged, and behaves accordingly. Legislators rush to pass bills outlawing boycotts, not only in obvious violation of the same freedoms those legislators are sworn to protect, but also a practical impossibility, this quest to stop people from not buying something. Terms like "economic terrorism" are tossed around by the same people who are quite happy to pull their donations from universities and literary festivals and anywhere that doesn't sufficiently silence whatever voices they want silenced. University administrators express shock at the utter inappropriateness of students' demands to cut ties with weapons makers and institutes complicit with occupation, and punish those students by withholding their degrees.

The idea that walking away is childish and unproductive is predicated on the inability to imagine anything but a walking away from, never a walking away toward—never that there might exist another destination. The walking away is not nihilism, it's not cynicism, it's not doing nothing—it's a form of engagement more honest, more soul-affirming, than anything the system was ever prepared to offer.

■

In the summer of 2005 I lucked into my first newspaper job. On the eve of graduating college, I applied for an internship at *The Globe and Mail* in Toronto. Every year the paper takes a crop of summer interns, and these are among the most sought-after positions in the somewhat claustrophobic world of Canadian journalism. Right around the time of my interview, the paper's investment reporter decided to take parental leave for the summer. I was hired and assigned his beat. I knew nothing about investment. My sole financial instrument was a checking account that, if I remember correctly, had about five and a half dollars in it the day I showed up to work.

Over the next ten years, I'd occasionally venture away from and then return to the paper's business section, in various guises, finally as a technology reporter. It was a strange job: I despised it, most of the time, or if not despised it, was certainly apathetic to both the industry and its self-congratulatory bloat. This was during one of those sporadic periods of collective tech sector insanity, when even a vague, plainly unworkable notion of a product or service could lure obscene sums from investors.

Once I traveled to Orlando to cover the annual BlackBerry major purchasers' conference (the company was still called Research In Motion back then, still flush with cash). It was a mostly pointless assignment, this conference designed to wine and dine the people who bought BlackBerrys by the thousands on behalf of companies or countries. In one of the more surreal evenings of my reporting life, I was shuttled to Universal Studios alongside a few dozen of these people, for an evening of liquor and roller coasters. It was an unsurprisingly bad combination—I remember watching a representative of the government of Mexico puke all over a pristine bit of shrubbery. Luckily for that man, not many people saw it—the company had rented out the entire theme park.

What sticks with me most from those years covering the business world is a kind of shared delusion, this sense that all of this wasn't just going to carry on forever, but continually improve. It is, of course, the delusion at the heart of capitalism, the existence of some essential, infinite wellspring of innovation and efficiency such as to make the prospect of equally infinite growth possible. But it's one thing to contend with this sort of thing in the abstract, another to sit opposite the cofounder of what was one of the biggest technology companies on the planet and hear him tell you, with a conviction I have never once mustered for any issue or argument, that this new tablet is going to be an absolute sensation because, you see, it has a very slightly raised rubber edge that makes it possible to place it on the table upside down without damaging the screen. I came to see how cults take shape.

Regardless of what the active component of economic growth may be—innovation, efficiency, a slightly raised rubber edge—so often on these assignments I was faced with the likelihood that what fueled the engine now was a kind of negation. Interviewing one of Uber's earliest executives, who demonstrated the company's route-finding algorithms with the unbridled enthusiasm of a small child at Christmas, I couldn't help but think what this company had really innovated was not some brilliant new solution to the traveling salesman problem, but the establishment of a new, lower norm of employee treatment. Success, growth, profit came from taking what might at one time have been decent, stable jobs and rebranding them as side hustles. The brilliant business idea was persuading people to expect less. I recall the same sensation the day a business magazine I used to freelance for named its CEO of the year: an airline executive whose hallmark achievement was figuring out a way to offload his workers' pension and health benefits, thereby doing something truly spectacular to the company's financial fortunes.

Whatever late capitalism is, it seems to be careening into this embrace of growth by negation. Through that prism, it's hard not to see the advances in something like artificial intelligence less driven by technological breakthroughs as by a society that has, over years, over decades, become normalized to a greater and greater magnitude of both loneliness and theft, such that a sputtering algorithm badly trained on the stolen work of real human beings might be celebrated with a straight face as something approximating humanness. Under this ordering, it is not some corporation's increasing capacity for *better* that drives the extractive world, but everyone else's increasing tolerance for *worse*.

Unconfronted, this kind of negation will not remain confined to widgets or labor or even the economic world. When the bigger wildfires come—as they already have—the industries whose callous disregard helped bring this about will depend on our ever-growing tolerance for calamity. When climate change upends the lives of billions, our governments will depend on our ever-growing tolerance for violence against the hordes of nameless others to enact its cruelest, most violent fortressing. In time, negation becomes all there is. To walk away from this system is to speak the only language the system will ever understand.

Otherwise, there will be nothing left under this way of living. In the end we will be asked to normalize not just unlimited extraction and unlimited suffering but total absence, a hollow that will look an awful lot like the one we were asked to overlay onto the minimum-wage workers and the climate refugees and the victims of endless colonial wars and, yes, even those dead Palestinian children who, had they been allowed to live, might have done something terrible.

Just for a moment, cease to believe that this particular group of people are human.

■

There is a numb, overriding grief that colors life in the audience to a slaughter. And like all measures of grief, it is born not of some exotic incendiary impulse, but of the most plain, unadorned knowing.

I know now there are people, some of them once very dear to me, to whom I will never speak again so long as I can help it. It's the people who said nothing, who knew full well what was happening and said nothing because there was a personal risk to it, a chance of getting yelled at or, God forbid, a chance of professional ramifications. It's the people who dug deeply into the paramount importance of their own safety, their own convenience. I feel no anger toward these people, not even frustration or disappointment, simply a kind of psychological leavetaking, an unspoken goodbye.

There is another kind of grief, too. The pettiest, most insignificant kind. The night I won that literary prize was one of the finest of my professional life. I didn't deserve it, the other nominees had written better books. But I got to stand up onstage and I got to say a few words about my mother and father, the two people who hurtled alongside me through our myriad departures. It's affirming, especially to a fragile ego, to be feted and to attend festivals and sit on boards and *partake*. The university students who protested and were punished for it probably celebrated the day they got their acceptance letters, were once proud of getting into these schools. This notion that millions of people around the world are delighting in their severance from so much institutional machinery seems absurd. It hurts. It means absolutely nothing compared to the suffering of people whose entire lives have been destroyed by what the same machinery is happy to abide. But it hurts.

Everywhere there is a great rage simmering, boiling over, and everything feels like an argument. But there are no arguments to be had anymore. I traverse the days, send the air back and forth in the shape of words with this person or that. Some agree, some don't but are careful not to make things uncomfortable. Some seem to have no opinion at all, nothing they can't ditch or rearrange at a moment's notice. I'm reminded of what Susan Sontag is supposed to have said about the great lesson of the Second World War: that 10 percent of people are fundamentally good, 10 are fundamentally evil, and the other 80 swayable in either direction. I don't know if I agree. There are young people all over the West risking expulsion and defamation, risking their livelihoods, their entire careers, to protest the killing. There are Jews being arrested on the streets of Frankfurt, blocking Grand Central Station in New York, fighting for peace. There are Indigenous communities who have suffered the Western world's most unspeakable atrocities and still find the will to stand up for an occupied land on the other side of the planet, who recognize a thing for what it is. I think instead of Virginia Woolf's conversation with that lawyer over the images of the war's dead: I cannot argue with you, cannot convince you of anything, because when you and I look at these pictures we see, fundamentally, different things.

In the final moments of Aaron Bushnell's life, officers rush to the site of his burning. One asks for a fire extinguisher, another points his gun at the flames.

CHAPTER TEN

ARRIVAL

On the worst night of my life, my daughter woke up coughing. She was one and a half years old at the time, with an undiagnosed respiratory condition. She'd been sniffly for a couple of days, but the cold seemed to pass. On its heels, though, she started having trouble breathing. She woke up in the middle of the night, and in the way these kinds of parental instincts so often kick in, we decided right away to take her to the emergency room.

For the next two days, we sat by her bedside, tubes of medication and supplementary oxygen snaking to her forearm and her nose. I watched the little monitor that noted her blood oxygen level, which when we arrived at the hospital had dipped into the low 80s. Every time the number rose a single digit, I came to understand what true religious devotion might feel like. It remains, to this day, the most scared I've ever been. We had access to some of the best medical facilities in the world and the insurance to pay for them and in a few days she was fine and it was still the most scared I've ever been.

I don't know how to make a person care for someone other than their own. Some days I can't even do it myself.

■

It is a disorienting thing, to keep a ledger of atrocity, to write the ugliness of each day as it happens. The months smother the months, soon the years will smother the years. Killings that might have once made front-page news slowly submit to the law of diminishing returns—what is left to say but more dead, more dead? The stock market churns, the president steps aside, the future of the most powerful nation hangs by a thread. News is new, and whatever this is, it can no longer be called new. Maybe this is the truly weightless time, after the front page loses interest but before the history books arrive.

One day this will end. In liberation, in peace, or in eradication at a scale so overwhelming it resets history. It'll end when sanctions pile up high enough, or the political cost of occupation and apartheid proves debilitating. When finally there is no other means of preserving self-interest but to act, the powerful will act. The same people who did the killing and financed the killing and justified the killing and turned away from the killing will congratulate themselves on doing the right thing. It is very important to do the right thing, eventually.

When the time comes to assign blame, most of those to blame will be long gone. There will always be feigned shock at how bad things really were, how we couldn't have possibly known. There will be those who say it was all the work of a few bad actors, people who misled the rest of us well-meaning folks. Anything to avoid contending with the possibility that all this killing wasn't the result of a system abused, but a system functioning exactly as intended.

For many people, that will be enough—a return to some more tolerable standard of subjugation. But for many, it won't be, and the liberal class that acquiesced so begrudgingly to the least of measures will find that a sizable contingent who might have previously aligned with its ideals can no longer bring themselves to do so. Not after what has been done, what has been seen, what cannot be forgotten.

There will be more moments of terror, both state-sanctioned and coldly, brutally individual. Only some of these acts will be formally labeled terror, though, because in the hierarchy of the Western world—of the world entire—revenge is a carefully delineated thing, around which whole histories and peoples must be ordered to make certain violence regrettable but understandable and other violence savage and infinitely punishable. But none of this changes the reality that revenge has always been a universal resource. When the state enacts it, it will be deemed proportional and measured. When the individual does, it will mark a brand-new starting point of history and everyone who looks or sounds or in any way resembles the author of that violence will be commanded in perpetuity to condemn it, knowing full well no amount of condemnation will ever be enough.

One day there will be no more looking away. Looking

away from climate disaster, from the last rabid takings of
extractive capitalism, from the killing of the newly stateless.
One day it will become impossible to accept the assurances
of the same moderates who say with great conviction: Yes the
air has turned sour and yes the storms have grown beyond
categorization and yes the fires and the floods have made of life
a wild careen from one disaster to the next and yes millions die
from the heat alone and entire species are swept into extinction
daily and the colonized are driven from their land and the
refugees die in droves on the borders of the unsated side of the
planet and yes supply chains are beginning to come apart and
yes soon enough it'll come to our doorstep, even our doorstep
in this last coddled bastion of the very civilized world, when
one day we turn on the tap and nothing comes out and we visit
the grocery store and the shelves are empty and we must finally
face the reality of it as billions before us have been made to
face the reality of it but until then, until that very last moment,
it's important to understand that this really is the best way of
doing things. One day it will be considered unacceptable,
in the polite liberal circles of the West, not to acknowledge all
the innocent people killed in that long-ago unpleasantness.
The truth and reconciliation committees are coming. The land
acknowledgments are coming. The very sorry descendants are
coming. After all, grief in arrears is grief just the same. Entire
departments of postcolonial studies will churn out papers
interrogating the obliviousness that led us all to that very
dark place, as though no one had seen from the beginning

exactly what that place was, as though no one had screamed warnings at the top of their lungs back when there was time to do something. One day the social currency of liberalism will accept as legal tender the suffering of those they previously smothered in silence, turned away from in disgust as one does carrion on the roadside. Far enough gone, the systemic murder of a people will become safe enough to fit on a lawn sign. There's always room on a liberal's lawn.

One day there will be an accounting, even as so often those who did the worst things imaginable in the killing fields were allowed to meld back into polite society. The man who put the bullet in the little girl's head might return to coach Little League games. The patrol that opened fire on the starving civilians might meet up every now and then for karaoke nights, might celebrate what they did when it is still acceptable, but over the years grow quieter, and finally bond over a shared silence thicker than blood. The soldier who drove the tank over the handcuffed body, who heard the sound and felt the rupture, might come home to a high school sweetheart and get down on one knee and might have children of his own one day. People who proved themselves capable of the most monstrous things human beings can do to one another might be granted one final immunity, because what's the alternative? To look into a neighbor's eyes and see, barely visible, the kind of stain no amount of repentance will ever wash away? Who can live like that? Better to move on.

There will be people who never move on, who to the end of their lives struggle to unsee the image of the body turned to red paste, the child forced to eat animal feed, the bones pushing against the skin, the slow extinguishing of life at the hands of hunger, the older siblings who must tell the younger ones that everyone else is gone, the hastily dug graves vast against the horizon, like goose bumps on the flesh of the earth. And every time they hear a politician profess the supremacy of international law, of human rights, of equality for all, they will hear only the sounds of screaming.

And yet, against all this, one day things will change.

Alongside the ledger of atrocity, I keep another. The Palestinian doctor who would not abandon his patients, even as the bombs closed in. The Icelandic writer who raised money to get the displaced out of Gaza. The American doctors and nurses who risked their lives to go treat the wounded in the middle of a killing field. The puppet-maker who, injured and driven from his home, kept making dolls to entertain the children. The congresswoman who stood her ground in the face of censure, of constant vitriol, of her own colleagues' indifference. The protesters, the ones who gave up their privilege, their jobs, who risked something, to speak out. The people who filmed and photographed and documented all this, even as it happened to them, even as they buried their dead.

It is not so hard to believe, even during the worst of things, that courage is the more potent contagion. That there are more invested in solidarity than annihilation. That just as it has always been possible to look away, it is always possible to stop looking away. None of this evil was ever necessary. Some carriages are gilded and others lacquered in blood, but the same engine pulls us all. We dismantle it now, build another thing entirely, or we hurtle toward the cliff, safe in the certainty that, when the time comes, we'll learn to lay tracks on air.

A NOTE ABOUT THE AUTHOR

OMAR EL AKKAD is an author and journalist. He was born in Egypt, grew up in Qatar, moved to Canada as a teenager, and now lives in the United States. He is a two-time winner of both the Pacific Northwest Booksellers Association Award and the Oregon Book Award for fiction. His books have been translated into thirteen languages. His debut novel, *American War*, was named by the BBC as one of one hundred novels that shaped our world.

A NOTE ON THE TYPE

This book was set in Minion, a typeface produced by the Adobe Corporation specifically for the Macintosh personal computer and released in 1990. Designed by Robert Slimbach, Minion combines the classic characteristics of old-style faces with the full complement of weights required for modern typesetting.

Composed by North Market Street Graphics,
Lancaster, Pennsylvania

Printed and bound by Berryville Graphics,
Berryville, Virginia

Designed by Michael Collica